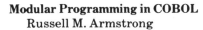

Modular Programming in COBOL
Russell M. Armstrong

Functional Analysis of Information Networks
Hal B. Becker

Functional Analysis of Information Processing
Grayce M. Booth

Effective Use of ANS COBOL Computer Programming Language
Laurence S. Cohn

The Database Administrator
John K. Lyon

Software Reliability: Principles and Practices
Glenford J. Myers

The Psychology of Business Systems
William C. Ramsgard

The Art of Software Testing
Glenford J. Myers

The Art of
Software Testing

Other books by
GLENFORD J. MYERS

Reliable Software Through Composite Design, 1975
Software Reliability: Principles and Practices, 1976
Composite/Structured Design, 1978
Advances in Computer Architecture, 1978

The Art of
Software Testing

Glenford J. Myers

Senior Staff Member
IBM Systems Research Institute

Lecturer in Computer Science
Polytechnic Institute of New York

A WILEY-INTERSCIENCE PUBLICATION

JOHN WILEY & SONS

New York · Chichester · Brisbane · Toronto · Singapore

Library of Congress Cataloging in Publication Data:

Myers, Glenford J   1946-
    The art of software testing.

    (Business data processing, a Wiley series)
    "A Wiley-Interscience publication."
    Includes bibliographies and index.
    1. Computer programs—Testing.   2. Debugging in
computer science.   I. Title.
QA76.6.M888   001.6'425   78-12923
ISBN 0-471-04328-1

Printed in the United States of America

30 29 28 27 26 25 24 23 22 21

To
Barbara & Janet

Preface

It has been known for some time that, in a typical programming project, approximately 50% of the elapsed time and over 50% of the total cost are expended in testing the program or system being developed. Given this knowledge, one would expect that program testing would have by now been refined into an "exact science," but this is far from the actual case. In fact, less seems to be known about software testing than about any other aspect of software development. Furthermore, testing has been an "out-of-vogue" subject, meaning that there is a sparcity of literature on the topic.

This may seem to be ample motivation for writing a book entitled *The Art of Software Testing,* but there was additional motivation. At various times, professors and teaching assistants have told me that "Our students graduate and move into industry without any substantial knowledge of how to go about testing a program. Moreover, we rarely have any advice to provide in our introductory courses on how a student should go about testing and debugging his or her exercises."

Hence, the purpose of this book is to fill these knowledge gaps, both for the professional programmer and the student of computer science. As the title implies, the book is a practical, rather than theoretical, discussion of the subject. Although it is possible to discuss program testing in a theoretical vein, the book is intended to be a practical, "both feet on the ground" handbook. Hence, many subjects related to program testing, such as the idea of mathematically proving the correctness of a program, were purposely excluded.

Chapter 1 is a short self-assessment test that every reader should take before reading further. It turns out that the most important practical information that one must understand about program testing is a set of philosophical and economic issues;

these are discussed in Chapter 2. Chapter 3 discusses the important concept of non-computer-based code walkthroughs or inspections. Rather than focus attention on the procedural or managerial aspects of this concept as most discussions do, Chapter 3 discusses it from a technical, how-to-find-errors point of view.

The knowledgeable reader will realize that the most important component in the bag of tricks of a program tester is the knowledge of how to write effective test cases; this is the subject of Chapter 4. Chapters 5 and 6 discuss, respectively, the testing of individual modules or subroutines and the testing of larger entities, with Chapter 7 presenting some practical advice on program debugging. Chapter 8 surveys testing tools, research areas, and techniques not discussed elsewhere in the book and contains an extensive bibliography.

The book has three major audiences. Although it is hoped that not everything in the book will be new information to the professional programmer, it should add to his or her knowledge of testing techniques. If the material allows one to detect just one more bug in one program, the price of the book will have been recovered many times over. The second audience is the project manager, since the book contains new, practical information on the management of the testing process. The third audience is the programming or computer-science student; the goal here is to expose the student to the problems of program testing and to provide a set of effective techniques. It is suggested that the book be used as a supplement in programming courses such that the student is exposed to the subject of software testing at an early time in his or her education.

GLENFORD J. MYERS

New York, New York
July 1978

Contents

The Art of
Software Testing

A Self-Assessment Test

Before beginning the book, it is strongly recommended that you take the following short test. The problem is the testing of the following program:

> The program reads three integer values from a card. The three values are interpreted as representing the lengths of the sides of a triangle. The program prints a message that states whether the triangle is scalene, isosceles, or equilateral.

On a sheet of paper, write a set of test cases (i.e., specific sets of data) that you feel would adequately test this program. When you have completed this, turn the page to analyze your tests.

The next step is an evaluation of the effectiveness of your testing. It turns out that this program is more difficult to write than it first appears to be. As a result, different versions of this program have been studied, and a list of common errors has been compiled. Evaluate your set of test cases by using it to answer the following questions. Give yourself one point for each "yes" answer.

1. Do you have a test case that represents a *valid* scalene triangle? (Note that test cases such as 1,2,3 and 2,5,10 do not warrant a "yes" answer, because there does not exist a triangle having such sides.)
2. Do you have a test case that represents a valid equilateral triangle?
3. Do you have a test case that represents a valid isosceles triangle? (A test case specifying 2,2,4 would not be counted.)
4. Do you have at least three test cases that represent valid isosceles triangles such that you have tried all three permutations of two equal sides (e.g., 3,3,4; 3,4,3; and 4,3,3)?
5. Do you have a test case in which one side has a zero value?
6. Do you have a test case in which one side has a negative value?
7. Do you have a test case with three integers greater than zero such that the sum of two of the numbers is equal to the third? (That is, if the program said that 1,2,3 represents a scalene triangle, it would contain a bug.)
8. Do you have at least three test cases in category 7 such that you have tried all three permutations where the length of one side is equal to the sum of the lengths of the other two sides (e.g., 1,2,3; 1,3,2; and 3,1,2)?
9. Do you have a test case with three integers greater than zero such that the sum of two of the numbers is less than the third (e.g., 1,2,4 or 12,15,30)?
10. Do you have at least three test cases in category 9 such that you have tried all three permutations (e.g., 1,2,4; 1,4,2; and 4,1,2)?
11. Do you have a test case in which all sides are 0 (i.e., 0,0,0)?
12. Do you have at least one test case specifying noninteger values?
13. Do you have at least one test case specifying the wrong number of values (e.g., two, rather than three, integers)?
14. For each test case, did you specify the expected output from the program in addition to the input values?

Of course, a set of test cases that satisfies the above conditions does not guarantee that all possible errors would be found, but since questions 1–13 represent errors that have actually occurred in different versions of this program, an adequate test of this program should expose these errors. If you are typical, you have done poorly on this test. As a point of reference, highly experienced professional programmers score, on the average, only 7.8 out of a possible 14. The point of the exercise is to illustrate that the testing of even a trivial program such as this is not an easy task. And if this is true, consider the difficulty of testing a 100,000-statement air-traffic-control system, a compiler, or even a mundane payroll program.

CHAPTER 2

The Psychology and Economics of Program Testing

Although one can discuss the subject of testing from several technical points of view, it appears that the most important considerations in software testing are issues of economics and human psychology. In other words, such considerations as the feasibility of "completely" testing a program, knowing who should test a program, and adopting the appropriate frame of mind toward testing appear to contribute more toward successful testing than do the purely technological considerations. Hence it is appropriate that we begin with these issues before moving on to matters of a more technical nature.

In considering these issues of economics and psychology, the most important single thing that one can learn about testing can be said at this point, and it will take only a few pages to do so. Once this consideration has been dealt with, everything else that can be discussed about program testing is merely supportive in nature and icing on the cake.

This vital consideration, one that seems almost trivial in nature, is the definition of the word "testing." The premise of this discussion is that most people use a totally incorrect definition of the word, and that this is the primary cause for poor program testing. Examples of these definitions are such statements as "Testing is the process of demonstrating that errors are not present," "The purpose of testing is to show that a program performs its intended functions correctly," and "Testing is the process of establishing confidence that a program does what it is supposed to do."

These definitions are incorrect in that they describe almost the *opposite* of what testing should be viewed as. Forgetting the definitions for the moment, consider that when one tests a program, one wants to add some value to the program (i.e., since testing is a costly activity, one wants to recover some of this cost by increasing the worth of the program). Adding value means raising the quality or reliability of the program. Raising the reliability of the program means finding and removing errors. Hence one should not test a program to show that it works; rather, one should start with the assumption that the program contains errors (a valid assumption for almost any program) and then test the program to find as many of the errors as possible. Thus a more appropriate definition is:

Testing is the process of executing a program with the intent of finding errors.

At this point the discussion may sound like just a subtle game of semantics, but it has been observed to have a profound effect on testing success. Since human beings tend to be highly goal-oriented, establishing the proper goal has an important psychological effect. If our goal is to demonstrate that a program has no errors, then we shall subconsciously be steered toward this goal; that is, we shall tend to select test data that have a low probability of causing the program to fail. On the other hand, if our goal is to demonstrate that a program has errors, our test data will have a higher probability of finding errors. The latter approach will add more value to the program than the former.

This definition of testing has many implications, many of which are scattered throughout the book. For instance, it implies that testing is a *destructive* process, even a sadistic process, which explains why most people find it difficult. That is, most of our society has a constructive, rather than destructive, outlook on life. Most people are inclined toward making objects rather than ripping them apart. The definition also has implications for how test cases (test data) should be designed and for who should and who should not test a given program.

Another way of reinforcing the proper definition of testing is to analyze the use of the words "successful" and "unsuccessful," in particular their use by project managers in categorizing the results of test cases. Most project managers call a test case that did not find an error a "successful test run," whereas a test that discovers a new error is usually called "unsuccessful." This is often a sign that the wrong definition of testing is being used, for the word "successful" denotes an achievement and the word "unsuccessful" denotes something undesirable or disappointing. However, since a test case that does not find an error is largely a waste of time and money, the descriptor "successful" seems inappropriate. (The astute reader will realize that we can only safely make this observation based on hindsight, since we cannot be absolutely sure that a test case will not find an error before we try it. However, this issue will be discussed later.)

Likewise, a test case that finds a new error can hardly be considered unsuccessful; rather, it has proven to be a valuable investment. Therefore, another way of reinforcing the proper definition of testing is to reverse the common use of these terms. We shall say that a successful test case is one that finds an error, and that an unsuccessful test case is one that causes a program to produce the correct result.

Consider the analogy of a person visiting a doctor because of an overall feeling of malaise. If the doctor runs some laboratory tests that do not locate the problem, we do not call the laboratory tests "successful"; they were unsuccessful tests in that the patient's net worth has been reduced by the $40 laboratory charge, the patient is still ill, and the patient now questions the doctor's ability as a diagnostician. However, if a laboratory test determines that the patient has a peptic ulcer, the test is successful because the doctor can now begin the appropriate treatment. Hence, the medical profession seems to use these words in the proper sense. (The analogy, of course, is that we should think of the program, as we begin testing it, as the sick patient.)

Another problem with such definitions as "testing is the process of demonstrating that errors are not present" is that such a goal is impossible to achieve for virtually all programs, even trivial programs. (If this statement troubles you, trust it for now since it is discussed later in the chapter.) Again, psychological studies tell us that people perform poorly when they set out on a task that they know to be infeasible or impossible. For instance, if one were instructed to solve the crossword puzzle in the Sunday *New York Times* in 15 minutes, we would observe little, if any, progress after 10 minutes because the person would be resigned to the fact that the task seems impossible. If we asked for a solution in four hours, however, we would probably observe more progress in the initial 10 minutes. Defining program testing as the process of uncovering errors in a program makes it a feasible task, thus overcoming this psychological problem.

A third problem with the common definitions such as "testing is the process of demonstrating that a program does what it is supposed to do" is that programs that do what they are supposed to do can still contain errors. That is, an error is clearly present if a program does not do what it is supposed to do, but errors are also present *if a program does what it is not supposed to do.* Consider the triangle program of Chapter 1. Even if we could demonstrate that the program correctly distinguishes among all scalene, isosceles, and equilateral triangles, the program would still be in error if it does something that it is not supposed to do (i.e., if it said that 1,2,3 represents a scalene triangle or that 0,0,0 represents an equilateral triangle). We are more likely to discover the latter class of errors if we view program testing as the process of finding errors than if we view it as the process of showing that a program does what it is supposed to do.

To summarize this vital discussion, program testing is more properly viewed as the destructive process of trying to find the errors (whose presence is assumed) in a program. A successful test case is one that furthers progress in this direction by causing the program to fail. Of course, one eventually wants to use program testing to establish some degree of confidence that a program does what it is supposed to do and does not do what it is not supposed to do, but this purpose is best achieved by a diligent exploration for errors. Consider someone approaching you with the claim that "my program is perfect" (error free). The best way to establish some confidence in this claim is to try to refute it, that is, to try to find imperfections rather than just confirm that the program works correctly for some set of input data.

THE ECONOMICS OF TESTING

Given this definition of program testing, an appropriate next step is the determination of whether it is possible to test a program to find *all* of its errors. As will be shown, the answer is negative, even for trivial programs. In general, it is impractical, often impossible, to find all the errors in a program. This fundamental problem will, in turn, be seen to have implications on the economics of testing, assumptions that the tester will have to make about the program, and the manner in which test cases are designed.

Black-Box Testing

One way to examine this issue is to explore a testing strategy called *black-box, data-driven,* or *input/output-driven* testing. In using this strategy, the tester views the program as a black box. That is, the tester is completely unconcerned about the internal behavior and structure of the program. Rather, the tester is only interested in finding circumstances in which the program does not behave according to its specifications. Test data are derived solely from the specifications (i.e., without taking advantage of knowledge of the internal structure of the program).

If one wishes, using this approach, to find all errors in the program, the criterion is *exhaustive input testing.* Exhaustive input testing is the use of every possible input condition as a test case. The reason that this is a necessary criterion to find all errors is that, for instance, if one tried three equilateral-triangle test cases for the triangle program, that in no way guarantees the correct detection of all equilateral triangles. The program could contain a special check for values 3842,3842,3842 and denote such a triangle as a scalene triangle. Since the program is a black box, the only way to be sure of detecting the presence of such a statement is by trying every input condition.

To exhaustively test the triangle program, then, one would have to create test cases for all valid triangles up to whatever is the maximum integer size. This in itself is an astronomical number of test cases, but it is in no way exhaustive; it would not cause such errors to be found where the program said that $-3,4,5$ is a scalene triangle and that $2,A,2$ is an isosceles triangle. To be sure of finding all such errors, one has to test using not only all *valid* inputs, but all *possible* inputs. Hence, to test the triangle program exhaustively, one would have to produce virtually an infinite number of test cases.

If this sounds difficult, exhaustive input testing of larger programs is even more of a problem (if the reader will permit me the liberty of talking about "numbers greater than infinity"). Consider attempting an exhaustive black-box test of a Cobol compiler. Not only would one have to create test cases representing all valid Cobol programs (again, virtually an infinite number), but one would have to create test cases for all invalid Cobol programs (an infinite number) to ensure that the compiler detects them as being invalid. That is, the compiler has to be tested to ensure that it does not do what it is not supposed to do—for example, successfully compile a syntactically incorrect program. The problem is even worse for programs having a "memory" (e.g., operating systems, data base systems, airlines reservation systems). In such programs, the execution of a transaction (e.g., a job, a data base inquiry, a reservation for a plane flight) is dependent upon what happened earlier (i.e., previous transactions). Hence, not only would one have to try all unique valid and invalid transactions, but also all possible sequences of transactions.

This discussion shows that exhaustive input testing is impossible. Two implications of this are that (1) one cannot test a program to guarantee that it is error-free and (2) a fundamental consideration in program testing is one of economics. That is, since exhaustive testing is out of the question, the objective should be to maximize the yield on the testing investment (i.e., maximize the number of errors found by a finite number of test cases). Doing so will involve, among other things, being able to peer inside the program and making certain reasonable, but not air-tight, assumptions about the program (e.g., if the triangle program detects 2,2,2, as an equilateral triangle, it seems reasonable that it will do the same for 3,3,3). This will form part of the test-case design strategy in Chapter 4.

White-Box Testing

Another testing strategy, *white-box* or *logic-driven* testing, permits one to examine the internal structure of the program. In using this strategy, the tester derives test data from an examination of the program's logic (and often, unfortunately, at the neglect of the specification).

What we wish to do at this point is to establish, for this strategy, the analog to exhaustive input testing in the black-box approach. To the uninitiated, causing every statement in the program to execute at least once might appear to be the answer, but it is not difficult to show that this is highly inadequate. Without belaboring the point, since this matter is discussed in more depth in Chapter 4, the analog is usually considered to be *exhaustive path testing*. That is, if one executes, via test cases, all possible paths of control flow through the program, then possibly the program can be said to be completely tested.

There are two flaws in this statement, however. One is that the number of unique logic paths through a program is astronomically large. To see this, consider the trivial program represented in Figure 2.1. The diagram is a control-flow graph. Each node or circle represents a segment of statements that execute sequentially, possibly terminating with a branching statement. Each edge or arc represents a transfer of control (branch) between segments. The diagram, then, depicts perhaps a 10- to 20-statement program consisting of a DO loop that iterates up to 20 times. Within the body of the DO loop is a set of nested IF statements. Determining the number of unique logic paths is the same as determining the total number of unique ways of moving from point A to point B (assuming that all decisions in the program are independent from one another). This number is approximately 10^{14}, or 100 trillion. It is computed from $5^{20} + 5^{19} + \ldots + 5^{1}$, where 5 is the number of paths through the loop body. Since most people have a difficult time visualizing such a number, consider it this way: if one could write, execute, and verify a test case every five minutes, it would take approximately one billion years to try every path.

Of course, in actual programs every decision is not independent from every other decision, meaning that the number of possible execution paths would be somewhat less. On the other hand, actual programs are much larger than the simple program depicted by Figure 2.1. Hence, exhaustive path testing, like exhaustive input testing, appears to be impractical, if not impossible.

The second flaw in the statement that exhaustive path testing means a complete test is that every path in a program could be tested, yet the program might still be loaded with errors. There are three explanations for this. The first is that an exhaustive path test in no way guarantees that a program matches its specification. For instance, if one were asked to write an ascending-order sorting routine but mistakenly produced a descending-order sorting routine, exhaustive path testing would be of little value; the program still has one bug: it is the wrong program. Second, a program may be incorrect because of *missing paths.* Exhaustive path testing, of course, would not detect the absence of necessary paths. Third, an exhaustive path test might not uncover *data-sensitivity* errors. There are many examples of such errors, but a simple example should suffice. Suppose, in a program, one had to compare two numbers for convergence, that

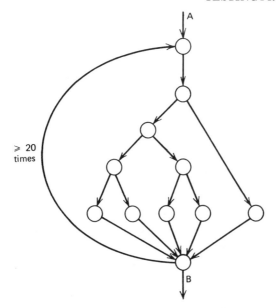

Figure 2.1   Control–flow graph of a small program.

is, to see if the difference between the two numbers is less than some predetermined value. One might write the statement as

    IF ((A-B) <EPSILON) ...

Of course the statement contains an error because it should compare EPSILON to the absolute value of A - B. Detection of this error, however, is dependent upon the values used for A and B and would not necessarily be detected by just executing every path through the program.

In conclusion, although exhaustive input testing is superior to exhaustive path testing, neither prove to be useful strategies because both are infeasible. Perhaps then, there are ways of combining elements of both black-box and white-box testing to derive a reasonable, but not air-tight, testing strategy. This matter is pursued further in Chapter 4.

TESTING PRINCIPLES

Continuing with the major premise of this chapter, that the most important considerations in software testing are issues of psychology, a set of vital testing principles or guidelines can be identified. These principles are interesting in that most of them appear to be intuitively obvious, yet they are all-too-often overlooked.

A necessary part of a test case is a definition of the expected output or result.

This obvious principle is one of the most frequent mistakes in program testing. Again, it is something that is based on human psychology. If the expected result of a test case has not been predefined, chances are that a plausible, but erroneous, result will be interpreted as a correct result because of the phenomenon of "the eye seeing what it wants to see." In other words, in spite of the proper destructive definition of testing, there is still a subconscious desire to see the correct result. One way of combating this is to encourage a detailed examination of all output by precisely spelling out, in advance, the expected output of the program. Therefore, a test case must consist of two components: a description of the input data to the program and a precise description of the correct output of the program for that set of input data.

The necessity of this is emphasized in a discussion by the logician Copi [1]:

> A problem may be characterized as a fact or group of facts for which we have no acceptable explanation, which seem unusual, or which fail to fit in with our expectations or preconceptions. It should be obvious that *some* prior beliefs are required if anything is to appear problematic. If there are no expectations, there can be no surprises.

A programmer should avoid attempting to test his or her own program.

This principle follows from earlier discussions in the chapter, principally the discussion that implied that testing is a destructive process. In other words, it is extremely difficult, after a programmer has been constructive while designing and coding a program, to suddenly, overnight, change his or her perspective and attempt to form a completely destructive frame of mind toward the program. As many homeowners know, removing wallpaper (a destructive process) is not easy, but it is almost unbearably depressing if you, rather than someone else, originally installed it. Hence most programmers cannot effectively test their own programs because they cannot bring themselves to form the necessary mental attitude: the attitude of wanting to expose errors.

In addition to this psychological problem, there is a second significant problem: the program may contain errors due to the programmer's misunderstanding of the problem statement or specification. If this is the case, it is likely that the programmer will have the same misunderstanding when attempting to test his or her own program.

Furthermore, testing can be viewed as being analogous to proofreading or writing a critique of a paper or book. As many writers are aware, it is extremely difficult to proofread and critique one's own work. That is, finding flaws in one's work seems counter to the human psyche.

This discussion does not mean to say that it is *impossible* for a programmer to test his or her own program, because, of course, programmers have had some success in testing their programs. Rather, it implies that testing is more effective and successful if performed by another party. Note that this argument does not apply to debugging (correcting known errors); debugging is more efficiently performed by the original programmer.

A programming organization should not test its own programs.

The argument here is similar to the previous argument. A project or programming organization is, in many senses, a living organism with similar psychological problems. Furthermore, in most environments, a programming organization or a project manager is largely measured on the ability to produce a program by a given date and for a certain cost. One reason for this is that it is easy to measure time and cost objectives, but it is extremely difficult to quantify the reliability of a program. Therefore it is difficult for a programming organization to be objective in testing its own program, because the testing process, if approached with the proper definition, may be viewed as decreasing the probability of meeting the schedule and cost objectives.

Again, this does not say that it is impossible for a programming organization to find some of its errors, for organizations do accomplish this with some degree of success. Rather, it implies that it is more economical for testing to be performed by some objective, independent party.

Thoroughly inspect the results of each test.

This is probably the most obvious principle, but again it is something that is often overlooked. In experiments performed by the author, many subjects failed to detect certain errors, even when symptoms of those errors were clearly observable on the output listings. It appears to be true that a significant percentage of errors that are eventually found are errors that were actually made visible by earlier test cases, but slipped by owing to failure to carefully inspect the results of those earlier test cases.

Test cases must be written for invalid and unexpected, as well as valid and expected, input conditions.

There is a natural tendency, when testing a program, to concentrate on the valid and expected input conditions, at the neglect of the invalid and unexpected conditions. For instance, this tendency has frequently appeared in the testing of the triangle program in Chapter 1. Few people, for instance, feed the program the numbers 1,2,5 to make sure that the program does not erroneously interpret this as a scalene triangle. Also, many errors that are suddenly discovered in production programs turn up when the program is used in some new or unexpected way. Therefore, test cases representing unexpected and invalid input conditions seem to have a higher error-detection yield than do test cases for valid input conditions.

Examining a program to see if it does not do what it is supposed to do is only half of the battle. The other half is seeing whether the program does what it is not supposed to do.

This is simply a corollary to the previous principle. It also implies that programs must be examined for unwanted side effects. For instance a payroll program that produces the correct paychecks is still an erroneous program if it also produces extra checks for nonexistent employees or if it overwrites the first record of the personnel file.

Avoid throw-away test cases unless the program is truly a throw-away program.

This problem is seen most often in the use of interactive systems to test programs. A common practice is to sit at a terminal, invent test cases on the fly, and then send these test cases through the program. The major problem is that test cases represent a valuable investment that, in this environment, disappears after the testing has been completed. Whenever the program has to be tested again (e.g., after correcting an error or making an improvement), the test cases will have to be reinvented. More often than not, since this reinvention requires a considerable amount of work, people tend to avoid it. Therefore the retest of the program is rarely as rigorous as the original test, meaning that if the modification causes a previously functional part of the program to fail, this error often goes undetected.

Do not plan a testing effort under the tacit assumption that no errors will be found.

This is a mistake often made by project managers and is a sign of the use of the incorrect definition of testing, that is, the assumption that testing is the process of showing that the program functions correctly.

The probability of the existence of more errors in a section of a program is proportional to the number of errors already found in that section.

This counterintuitive phenomenon is illustrated in Figure 2.2. At first glance it makes little sense, but it is a phenomenon that has been observed in many programs. For instance, if a program consists of two modules or subroutines A and B and one has found to date five errors in module A and only one error in mod-

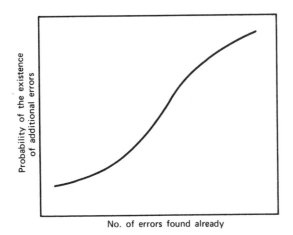

Figure 2.2 **The surprising errors–remaining/errors–found relationship.**

ule B, and if module A has not been purposely subjected to a more rigorous test, then this principle tells us that the likelihood of more errors in module A is greater than the likelihood of more errors in module B. Another way of stating it is that errors seem to come in clusters and that, in the typical program, some sections seem to be much more error prone than other sections, although nobody as yet has supplied a good explanation for why this occurs. As one example, the phenomenon has been observed in IBM's S/370 operating systems. In one of these operating systems, 47% of the APARs (errors found by users) were associated with only 4% of the modules within the system.

This phenomenon is useful in that it gives us insight or feedback in the testing process. If a particular section of a program seems to be much more error prone than other sections, then this phenomenon tells us that, in terms of yield on our testing investment, additional testing efforts are best focused against this error-prone section.

> *Testing is an extremely creative and intellectually challenging task.*

It is probably true that the creativity required in testing a large program exceeds the creativity required in designing that program. We have already seen that it is impossible to test a program such that the absence of all errors can be guaranteed. There are methodologies, which are discussed later in the book, that allow one to develop a reasonable set of test cases for a program, but these methodologies still require a significant amount of creativity.

To reemphasize some earlier thoughts in the chapter, we can conclude by listing three more important testing principles:

> *Testing is the process of executing a program with the intent of finding errors.*

> *A good test case is one that has a high probability of detecting an as-yet undiscovered error.*

> *A successful test case is one that detects an as-yet undiscovered error.*

REFERENCES

1. I. M. Copi, *Introduction to Logic.* New York: Macmillan, 1968.

CHAPTER **3**

Program Inspections, Walkthroughs, and Reviews

For many years, the majority of the programming community worked under the assumptions that programs are written solely for machine execution and are not intended to be read by people, and that the only way to test a program is by executing it on a machine. This attitude began to change in the early 1970s, largely as a result of Weinberg's *The Psychology of Computer Programming* [1]. Weinberg built a convincing argument for why programs should be read by people, and also indicated that this could be an effective error-detection process.

For this reason, the process of non-computer-based testing (or "human testing"), the subject of this chapter, is discussed before the more traditional computer-based testing techniques. Experience has shown that these "human testing" techniques are quite effective in finding errors, so much so that one or more of these should be employed in every programming project. The methods discussed herein are intended to be applied between the time that the program is coded and the time that computer-

17

based testing begins. Analogous methods can be developed and applied at earlier stages in the programming process (i.e., at the end of each design stage), but these are outside the scope of this book; references 2 and 3 discuss some of these methods.

One important note is warranted before discussing the methods. Because of their informal nature (informal with respect to other, more-formal methods such as mathematical proofs of program correctness, which are not yet practical enough to be discussed here), people's first reaction is often one of skepticism, feeling that something so simple and informal cannot be useful. However, use of the methods has shown that they do not "get in the way." Rather, they substantially contribute to productivity and reliability in two major ways. First, it is generally recognized that the earlier that errors are found, the lower are the costs of correcting the errors and the higher is the probability of correcting the errors correctly. Second, programmers seem to experience a psychological change when computer-based testing commences. Internally induced pressures seem to build rapidly and there is a tendency to want to "fix this darn bug as soon as possible." Because of these pressures, programmers tend to make more mistakes when correcting an error found during computer-based testing than they make when correcting an error found earlier.

INSPECTIONS AND WALKTHROUGHS

Code inspections and walkthroughs are the two primary "human testing" methods. Since the two methods have a lot in common, their similarities are discussed here. Their differences are discussed in the two subsequent sections.

Inspections and walkthroughs involve the reading or visual inspection of a program by a team of people. Hence they stem directly from the ideas of Weinberg [1]. Both methods involve some preparatory work by the participants. The climax is a "meeting of the minds," a conference held by the participants. The objective of the meeting is to find errors, but not to find solutions to the errors (i.e., to test but not to debug).

Inspections and walkthroughs have been widely used for some time now, but little work has been done in determining why they are successful. Not surprisingly, the reason for their success is related to some of the principles in Chapter 2. Note that the process is performed by a group of people (optimally three or four), only one of whom is the author of the program. Hence the program is essentially being tested by people other than the author, which is in consonance with the testing principle stating that an individual is usually ineffective in testing his or her own program. Also, people occasionally state that an inspection or walkthrough is simply a new name for the older "desk-checking" process (the process of a programmer reading his or her own program before testing it), but inspections and walkthroughs have been found to be far more effective, again because people other than the program's author are involved in the process. These processes also appear to result in lower debugging (error correction) costs, since, when they find an error, the precise nature of the error is usually located. In addition, they expose a *batch* of errors, thus allowing the errors to be corrected later en masse. Computer-based testing, on the other hand, normally exposes only a *symptom* of the error (e.g., the program does not terminate or the program prints a meaningless result), and errors are usually detected and corrected one by one.

Experience with these methods has found them to be effective in finding from 30% to 70% of the logic design and coding errors in typical programs. (They are not, however, effective in detecting "high-level" design errors, such as errors made in the requirements-analysis process.) For instance, a controlled experiment found that walkthroughs and inspections detected an average of 38% of the total errors in the program studied [4]. Uses of code inspections by IBM have shown error-detection efficiencies as high as 80% [5] (not 80% of *all* errors, because Chapter 2 tells us that we can never know the total number of errors in a program, but in this case 80% of all errors found by the end of the testing processes). Of course, a possible criticism of these statistics is that the human processes find only the "easy" errors (those that would be trivial to find with computer-based testing) and that the difficult, obscure, or tricky errors can only be found by computer-based testing. However, one study has found that this criticism is unsubstantiated [6]. Also, another study [4] has shown that the human processes tend to be *more* effective than the computer-based testing processes in finding *certain* types of errors, *while the opposite is true for other types of errors.* The implication is that inspections/walkthroughs and computer-based testing are complementary; error-detection efficiency will suffer if one or the other is not present.

Lastly, although these processes are invaluable for testing new programs, they are of equal, or even more, value in testing modifications to programs. Experience shows that modifying an existing program is a more error-prone process (in terms of errors per statement written) than writing a new program. Hence program modifications should also be subjected to these testing processes.

CODE INSPECTIONS

A code inspection is a set of procedures and error-detection techniques for group code reading [7]. Most discussions of code inspections focus on the procedures, forms to be filled out, and so on; here, after a short summary of the general procedure, we shall focus on the actual error-detection techniques.

An inspection team usually consists of four people. One of the four people plays the role of a moderator. The moderator is expected to be a competent programmer, but he or she is not the author of the program and need not be acquainted with the details of the program. The duties of the moderator include distributing materials for, and scheduling, the inspection session, leading the session, recording all errors found, and ensuring that the errors are subsequently corrected. Hence the moderator can be likened to a quality-control engineer. The second team member is the programmer. The remaining team members usually consist of the program's designer (if different from the programmer) and a test specialist.

The general procedure is the following. The moderator distributes the program's listing and design specification to the other participants well in advance of (e.g., several days before) the inspection session. The participants are expected to familiarize themselves with the material prior to the session. During the inspection session, two activities occur:

1. The programmer is requested to narrate, statement by statement, the logic of the program. During the discourse, questions are raised and pursued to determine if errors exist. Experience has shown that many of the errors discovered are actually found by the programmer, rather than the other team members, during the narration. In other words, the simple act of reading aloud one's program to an audience seems to be a remarkably effective error-detection technique.
2. The program is analyzed with respect to a checklist of historically common programming errors (such a checklist is discussed in the next section).

The moderator is responsible for ensuring that the discussions proceed along productive lines and that the participants focus their attention on finding errors, not correcting them. (The correction of errors is performed by the programmer after the inspection session.)

After the session, several things occur. The programmer is given a list of the errors found. If more than a few errors were found, or if an error was found that requires a substantial correction, arrangements might be made by the moderator to reinspect the program after the errors are corrected. The list of errors is also analyzed, categorized, and used to refine the error checklist to improve the effectiveness of future inspections.

Note that most descriptions of the inspection process state, as described above, that errors are not to be corrected during the inspection session. However, there is another view on this. At least one report [8] has indicated experience to the contrary:

> Instead of anyone at first noticing the basic problem with the design, someone would notice a minor problem. Two or three people, including the programmer responsible for the code, would then propose obvious patches to the design to handle this special case. The discussion of this minor problem would, however, have focused the group's attention on that particular area of the design. During the discussion of the best way to patch the design to handle this minor problem, someone would notice a second problem. Now that the group had seen two problems related to the same aspect of the design, comments would come thick and fast, with interruptions every few sentences. In a few minutes, this whole area of the design would be thoroughly explored and any problems would be obvious . . . As mentioned above, many major problems found during the flowchart reviews were discovered as a result of repeatedly unsuccessful attempts to resolve what first seemed to be trivial problems.

The time and location of the inspection must be planned to avoid all outside interruptions. The optimal amount of time for the inspection session appears to be from 90 to 120 minutes. Since the session is a mentally taxing experience, longer sessions tend to be less productive. Most inspections proceed at a rate of approximately 150 program statements per hour, implying that large programs must be examined by multiple inspections, each inspection perhaps dealing with one or several modules or subroutines.

Note that for the inspection process to be effective, the appropriate attitude must be established. If the programmer views the inspection as an attack on his or her character and hence adopts a defensive posture, the process will be ineffective. Rather, the programmer must approach the process with an "egoless" attitude [1]; the programmer must view the process in a positive and constructive light: the objective of the inspection is to find errors in the program, thus improving the quality of his or her work. For this reason, most people recommend that the results of an inspection be a confidential matter, shared only among the participants. In particular, the use of inspection results by managers can quickly defeat the purpose of the process.

The inspection process also has several beneficial side effects in addition to its main effect of finding errors. In addition to seeing the errors made and hopefully learning from these mistakes, the programmer usually receives feedback concerning his or her programming style and choice of algorithms and programming techniques. The other participants gain in a similar way by being exposed to another programmer's errors and programming style. Lastly, the inspection process is a way of identifying early the most error-prone sections of the program, thus allowing one to focus more attention on these sections during the computer-based testing processes (one of the testing principles of Chapter 2).

AN ERROR CHECKLIST FOR INSPECTIONS

An important part of the inspection process is the use of a checklist to examine the program for common errors. Unfortunately, suggested checklists (e.g., reference 9) often concentrate more on issues of style than on errors (e.g., "Are comments accurate and meaningful?" and "Are THEN/ELSE and DO/END groups aligned?") and the error checks are too nebulous to be useful (e.g., "Does the code do what the design called for?"). The checklist in this section was compiled by the author after many years of study of software errors. The checklist is largely language independent, meaning that most of the errors can occur with any programming language. The reader may wish to supplement this list with errors peculiar to his programming language and with errors detected after using the inspection process.

Data-Reference Errors

1. Is a variable referenced whose value is unset or uninitialized? This is probably the most frequent programming error; it occurs in a wide variety of circumstances. For each

reference to a data item (e.g., variable, array element, field in a structure), attempt to "prove" informally that the item has a value at that point.

2. For all array references, is each subscript value within the defined bounds of the corresponding dimension?

3. For all array references, does each subscript have an integer value? This is not necessarily an error in all languages, but it is a dangerous practice.

4. For all references through pointer or reference variables, is the referenced storage currently allocated? This is known as the "dangling reference" problem. It occurs in situations where the lifetime of a pointer is greater than the lifetime of the referenced storage. One situation occurs where a pointer references a local variable within a procedure, the pointer value is assigned to an output parameter or a global variable, the procedure returns (freeing the referenced storage), and later the program attempts to use the pointer value. In a manner similar to checking for the prior errors, try to prove informally that, in each reference using a pointer variable, the referenced storage exists.

5. When a storage area has alias names with differing attributes, does the data value in this area have the correct attributes when referenced via one of these names? Situations to look for are the use of the DEFINED attribute or based storage in PL/I, the EQUIVALENCE statement in Fortran, and the REDEFINES clause in Cobol. As an example, a Fortran program contains a real variable A and an integer variable B; both are made aliases for the same storage area by using an EQUIVALENCE statement. If the program stores a value into A and then references variable $B,$ an error is likely to be present since the machine would use the floating-point bit representation in the storage area as an integer.

6. Does a variable's value have a type or attribute other than that expected by the compiler? This situation might occur where a PL/I or Cobol program reads a record into storage and references it by using a structure, but the physical representation of the record differs from the structure definition.

7. Are there any explicit or implicit addressing problems if, on the machine being used, the units of storage allocation are smaller than the units of storage addressability? For instance, in PL/I on the IBM S/370, fixed-length bit strings do

not necessarily begin on byte boundaries, but addresses only point to byte boundaries. If a program computes the address of a bit string and later refers to the string through this address, the wrong storage may be referenced. This situation could also occur when passing a bit-string argument to a subroutine.

8. If pointer or reference variables are used, does the referenced storage have the attributes expected by the compiler? An example of such an error is where a PL/I pointer, upon which a data structure is based, is assigned the address of a different data structure.

9. If a data structure is referenced in multiple procedures or subroutines, is the structure defined identically in each procedure?

10. When indexing into a string, are the limits of the string exceeded?

11. Are there any "off by one" errors in indexing operations or in subscript references to arrays?

Data-Declaration Errors

1. Have all variables been explicitly declared? A failure to do so is not necessarily an error, but it is a common source of trouble. For instance, if a Fortran subroutine receives an array parameter and fails to define the parameter as an array (e.g., in a DIMENSION statement), a reference to the array [e.g., X=A (I)] is interpreted as a function call, leading to the machine's attempting to execute the array as a program. If a variable is not explicitly declared in an inner procedure or block, is it understood that the variable is shared with the enclosing block?

2. If all attributes of a variable are not explicitly stated in the declaration, are the defaults well understood? For instance, the default attributes received in PL/I are often a source of surprise.

3. Where a variable is initialized in a declarative statement, is it properly initialized? In many languages, initialization of arrays and strings is somewhat complicated and hence error prone.

4. Is each variable assigned the correct length, type, and storage class (e.g., STATIC, AUTOMATIC, BASED, or CONTROLLED in PL/I)?

5. Is the initialization of a variable consistent with its storage

type? For instance, if a variable in a Fortran subroutine needs to be reinitialized each time the subroutine is called, it must be initialized with an assignment statement rather than a DATA statement. If a PL/I declaration initializes a variable, and if the initialization is to be done each time the procedure is called, the variable's storage class should be stated as AUTOMATIC rather than STATIC.

6. Are there any variables with similar names (e.g., VOLT and VOLTS)? This is not necessarily an error, but it is a sign that the names may have been confused somewhere within the program.

Computation Errors

1. Are there any computations using variables having inconsistent (e.g., nonarithmetic) data types?
2. Are there any mixed-mode computations? An example is the addition of a floating-point variable to an integer variable. Such occurrences are not necessarily errors, but they should be explored carefully to ensure that the language's conversion rules are understood. This is extremely important in a language with complicated conversion rules (e.g., PL/I). For instance, the following PL/I program fragment:

```
DECLARE A BIT (1);
A=1;
```

leaves A with the bit value 0, not 1.

3. Are there any computations using variables having the same data type but different lengths? This question is applicable to PL/I and derivations thereof. For instance, the result of the PL/I expression $25+1/3$ is $5.333\ldots$, not $25.333\ldots$
4. Is the target variable of an assignment smaller than the right-hand expression?
5. Is an overflow or underflow exception possible during the computation of an expression? That is, the end result may appear to have a valid value, but an intermediate result might be too big or too small for the machine's data representations.
6. Is it possible for the divisor in a division operation to be zero?
7. If the underlying machine represents variables in base-2

form, are there any consequences of the resulting inaccuracy? That is, 10×0.1 is rarely equal to 1.0 on a binary machine.

8. Where applicable, can the value of a variable go outside its meaningful range? For example, statements assigning a value to the variable PROBABILITY might be checked to ensure than the assigned value will always be positive and not greater than 1.0.

9. For expressions containing more than one operator, are the assumptions about the order of evaluation and precedence of operators correct?

10. Are there any invalid uses of integer arithmetic, particularly divisions? For instance, if I is an integer variable, whether the expression $2*I/2$ is equal to I depends on whether I has an odd or an even value and whether the multiplication or division is performed first.

Comparison Errors

1. Are there any comparisons between variables having inconsistent data types (e.g., comparing a character string to an address)?

2. Are there any mixed-mode comparisons or comparisons between variables of different lengths? If so, ensure that the conversion rules are well understood.

3. Are the comparison operators correct? Programmers frequently confuse such relationships as *at most, at least, greater than, not less than, less than or equal.*

4. Does each Boolean expression state what it is supposed to state? Programmers often make mistakes when writing logical expressions involving "and," "or," and "not."

5. Are the operands of a Boolean operator Boolean? Have comparison and Boolean operators been erroneously mixed together? This represents another frequent class of mistakes. Examples of a few typical mistakes are illustrated below. If one wants to determine whether I is between 2 and 10, the expression $2<I<10$ is incorrect; instead, it should be $(2<I)$ & $(I<10)$. If one wants to determine if I is greater than X or Y, $I>X|Y$ is incorrect; instead, it should be $(I>X)|(I>Y)$. If one wants to compare three numbers for equality, $IF(A=B=C)$ does something quite different. If one wishes to test the mathematical relation $X > Y > Z$, the correct expression is $(X>Y)\&(Y>Z)$.

6. Are there any comparisons between fractional or floating-point numbers that are represented in base-2 by the underlying machine? This is an occasional source of errors because of truncation and base-2 approximations of base-10 numbers.

7. For expressions containing more than one Boolean operator, are the assumptions about the order of evaluation and the precedence of operators correct? That is, if you see an expression such as (A=2)&(B=2)I(C=3), is it well understood whether the *and* or the *or* is performed first?

8. Does the way in which your compiler evaluates Boolean expressions affect the program? For instance the statement

IF(X≠0)&((Y/X)>Z)

is acceptable for some PL/I compilers (i.e., compilers that end the test as soon as one side of an *and* is false), but causes a division by 0 when compiled with other compilers.

Control-Flow Errors

1. If the program contains a multiway branch (e.g., a computed GO TO in Fortran), can the index variable ever exceed the number of branch possibilities? For example, in the Fortran statement

GO TO (200,300,400), I

will *I* always have the value 1, 2, or 3?

2. Will every loop eventually terminate? Devise an informal proof or argument showing that each loop will terminate.

3. Will the program, module, or subroutine eventually terminate?

4. Is it possible that, because of the conditions upon entry, a loop will never execute? If so, does this represent an oversight? For instance, for loops headed by the following statements:

DO WHILE (NOTFOUND)
DO I=X TO Z

what happens if NOTFOUND is initially *false* or if X is greater than Z?

5. For a loop controlled by both iteration and a Boolean condi-

tion (e.g., a searching loop), what are the consequences of "loop fallthrough"? For example, for a loop headed by

DO I = 1 TO TABLESIZE WHILE (NOTFOUND)

what happens if NOTFOUND never becomes false?

6. Are there any "off by one" errors (e.g., one too many or too few iterations)?

7. If the language contains a concept of statement groups (e.g., DO/END groups in PL/I), is there an explicit END for each group and do the ENDs correspond to their appropriate groups?

8. Are there any nonexhaustive decisions? For instance, if an input parameter's expected values are 1, 2, or 3, does the logic assume that it must be 3 if it is not 1 or 2? If so, is the assumption valid?

Interface Errors

1. Does the number of parameters received by this module equal the number of arguments sent by each of the calling modules? Also, is the order correct?

2. Do the attributes (e.g., type and size) of each parameter match the attributes of each corresponding argument?

3. Does the units system of each parameter match the units system of each corresponding argument? For example, is the parameter expressed in degrees but the argument expressed in radians?

4. Does the number of arguments transmitted by this module to another module equal the number of parameters expected by that module?

5. Do the attributes of each argument transmitted to another module match the attributes of the corresponding parameter in that module?

6. Does the units system of each argument transmitted to another module match the units system of the corresponding parameter in that module?

7. If built-in functions are invoked, are the number, attributes, and order of the arguments correct?

8. If a module has multiple entry points, is a parameter ever referenced that is not associated with the current point of

entry? Such an error exists in the second assignment statement in the following PL/I program:

```
A:  PROCEDURE(W,X);
    W=X+1;
    RETURN;
B:  ENTRY (Y,Z);
    Y=X+Z;
    END;
```

9. Does a subroutine alter a parameter that is intended to be
    only an input value?
10. If global variables are present (e.g., PL/I variables having
    the EXTERNAL attribute, variables listed in a Fortran
    COMMON statement), do they have the same definition and
    attributes in all modules that reference them?
11. Are constants ever passed as arguments? In some Fortran
    implementations a statement such as

```
CALL SUBX (J,3)
```

is dangerous, since if the subroutine SUBX assigns a value
to its second parameter, the value of the constant 3 will be
altered.

Input/Output Errors

1. If files are explicitly declared, are their attributes correct?
2. Are the attributes on the OPEN statement correct?
3. Does the format specification agree with the information in
    the I/O statement? For instance, in Fortran, does each FOR-
    MAT statement agree (in terms of the number and attrib-
    utes of the items) with the corresponding READ or WRITE
    statement? The same applies to the correspondence between
    a data list and a format list in a PL/I I/O statement.
4. Is the size of the I/O area in storage equal to the record size?
5. Have all files been opened before use?
6. Are end-of-file conditions detected and handled correctly?
7. Are I/O error conditions handled correctly?
8. Are there spelling or grammatical errors in any text that is
    printed or displayed by the program?

Other Checks

1. If the compiler produces a cross-reference listing of identifiers, examine it for variables that are never referenced or referenced only once.
2. If the compiler produces an attribute listing, check the attributes of each variable to ensure that no unexpected default attributes have been assigned.
3. If the program compiled successfully, but the compiler produced one or more "warning" or "informational" messages, check each one carefully. Warning messages are indications

---

DATA REFERENCE

1. Unset variables used?
2. Subscripts within bounds?
3. Noninteger subscripts?
4. Dangling references?
5. Correct attributes when aliasing?
6. Record and structure attributes match?
7. Computing addresses of bit strings? Passing bit-string arguments?
8. Based storage attributes correct?
9. Structure definitions match across procedures?
10. String limits exceeded?
11. Off-by-one errors in indexing or subscripting operations?

DATA DECLARATION

1. All variables declared?
2. Default attributes understood?
3. Arrays and strings initialized properly?
4. Correct lengths, types, and storage classes assigned?
5. Initialization consistent with storage class?
6. Any variables with similar names?

COMPUTATION

1. Computations on nonarithmetic variables?
2. Mixed-mode computations?
3. Computations on variables of different lengths?
4. Target size less than size of assigned value?
5. Intermediate result overflow or underflow?
6. Division by zero?
7. Base-2 inaccuracies?
8. Variable's value outside of meaningful range?
9. Operator precedence understood?
10. Integer divisions correct?

COMPARISON

1. Comparisons between inconsistent variables?
2. Mixed-mode comparisons?
3. Comparison relationships correct?
4. Boolean expressions correct?
5. Comparison and Boolean expressions mixed?
6. Comparisons of base-2 fractional values?
7. Operator precedence understood?
8. Compiler evaluation of Boolean expressions understood?

Figure 3.1   **Inspection error-checklist summary, part 1.**

that the compiler suspects that you are doing something of questionable validity; all of these suspicions should be reviewed. Informational messages may list undeclared variables or language uses that impede code optimization.

4. Is the program or module sufficiently robust? That is, does it check its input for validity?

5. Is there function missing from the program?

The checklist is summarized in Figures 3.1 and 3.2.

WALKTHROUGHS

The code walkthrough, like the inspection, is a set of procedures and error-detection techniques for group code reading. It shares much in common with the inspection process, but the procedures are slightly different, and a different error-detection technique is employed.

Like the inspection, the walkthrough is an uninterrupted meeting of one to two hours in duration. The walkthrough team consists of three to five people. One of these people plays a role similar to that of the moderator in the inspection process, another person plays the role of a secretary (a person who records all errors found), and a third person plays the role of a "tester." Suggestions as to who the three to five people should be vary. Of course, the programmer is one of these people. Suggestions for the other participants include (1) a highly experienced programmer, (2) a programming-language expert, (3) a new programmer (to give a fresh, unbiased outlook), (4) the person who will eventually maintain the program, (5) someone from a different project, and (6) someone from the same programming team as the programmer.

The initial procedure is identical to that of the inspection process: the participants are given the materials several days in advance to allow them to "bone up" on the program. However, the procedure in the meeting is different. Rather than simply reading the program or using error checklists, the participants "play computer." The person designated as the tester comes to the meeting armed with a small set of paper test cases—representative sets of inputs (and expected outputs) for the program or module. During the meeting, each test case is mentally executed. That is, the test data are walked through the logic of the program. The state of the program (i.e., the values of the variables) is monitored on paper or a blackboard.

CONTROL FLOW

1. Multiway branches exceeded?
2. Will each loop terminate?
3. Will program terminate?
4. Any loop bypasses because of entry conditions?
5. Are possible loop fallthroughs correct?
6. Off-by-one iteration errors?
7. DO/END statements match?
8. Any nonexhaustive decisions?

INTERFACES

1. Number of input parameters equal to number of arguments?
2. Parameter and argument attributes match?
3. Parameter and argument units system match?
4. Number of arguments transmitted to called modules equal to number of parameters?
5. Attributes of arguments transmitted to called modules equal to attributes of parameters?
6. Units system of arguments transmitted to called modules equal to units system of parameters?
7. Number, attributes, and order of arguments to built-in functions correct?
8. Any references to parameters not associated with current point of entry?
9. Input-only arguments altered?
10. Global variable definitions consistent across modules?
11. Constants passed as arguments?

INPUT/OUTPUT

1. File attributes correct?
2. OPEN statements correct?
3. Format specification matches I/O statement?
4. Buffer size matches record size?
5. Files opened before use?
6. End-of-file conditions handled?
7. I/O errors handled?
8. Any textual errors in output information?

OTHER CHECKS

1. Any unreferenced variables in cross-reference listing?
2. Attribute list what was expected?
3. Any warning or informational messages?
4. Input checked for validity?
5. Missing function?

Figure 3.2   **Inspection error-checklist summary, part 2.**

Of course, the test cases must be simple in nature and few in number, because people "execute" programs at a rate that is many orders of magnitude slower than a machine. Hence, the test cases themselves do not play a critical role; rather, they serve as a vehicle for getting started and for questioning the programmer about his or her logic and assumptions. In most walkthroughs, more errors are found during the process of questioning the programmer than are found directly by the test cases themselves.

As in the inspection, the attitude of the participants is crucial. Comments should be directed toward the program rather than the programmer. In other words, errors are not viewed as weaknesses in the person who committed them. Rather, they are viewed as being inherent in the difficulty of program development and as a result of the as-yet primitive nature of current programming methods.

The walkthrough should have a follow-up process similar to that described for the inspection process. Also, the side effects observed from inspections (identification of error-prone sections and education in errors, style, and techniques) also apply to the walkthrough process.

DESK CHECKING

A third human error-detection process is the older practice of desk checking. A desk check can be viewed as a one-person inspection or walkthrough; a person reads a program, checks it with respect to an error list, and/or walks test data through it.

For most people, desk checking is relatively unproductive. One reason is that it is a completely undisciplined process. A second, and more important, reason is that it runs counter to a testing principle of Chapter 2—the principle that people are generally ineffective in testing their own programs. For this reason, one could deduce that desk checking is best performed by a person other than the author of the program (e.g., two programmers might swap programs rather than desk check their own programs), but even this is less effective than the walkthrough or inspection process. The reason is the synergistic effect of the walkthrough or inspection team. The team session fosters a healthy environment of competition; people like to show off by finding errors. In a desk checking process, since there is no one to whom one can show off, this apparently valuable effect is missing. In short, desk checking may be more valuable than doing nothing at all, but it is much less effective than the inspection or walkthrough.

PEER RATINGS

The last human-review process is not associated with program testing (i.e., its objective is not to find errors). This process is included here, however, because it is related to the idea of code reading.

Peer rating [10] is a technique of evaluating anonymous programs in terms of their overall quality, maintainability, extensibility, usability, and clarity. The purpose of the technique is to provide programmer self-evaluation.

A programmer is selected to serve as an administrator of the process. The administrator, in turn, selects approximately 6–20 participants (6 is the minimum to preserve anonymity). The participants are expected to have similar backgrounds (e.g., one should not group Cobol application programmers with assembly-language system programmers). Each participant is asked to select two of his own programs to be reviewed. One should be representative of what he considers to be his finest work; the other should be a program that the programmer considers to be poorer in quality.

Once the programs have been collected, they are randomly distributed to the participants. Each participant is given four programs to review. Two of the programs are "finest" programs, and two are "poorer" programs, but the reviewer is not told which is which. Each participant spends 30 minutes with each program and then completes an evaluation form after reviewing the program. After reviewing all four programs, each participant rates the relative quality of the four programs. The evaluation form asks the reviewer to answer, on a scale from 1 to 7 (1 meaning definitely "yes," 7 meaning definitely "no"), such questions as:

Was the program easy to understand?
Was the high-level design visible and reasonable?
Was the low-level design visible and reasonable?
Would it be easy for you to modify this program?
Would you be proud to have written this program?

The reviewer is also asked for general comments and suggested improvements.

After the review, the participants are given the anonymous evaluation forms for their two contributed programs. The participants are also given a statistical summary showing the overall and detailed ranking of their original programs across the entire set of programs, as well as an analysis of how their ratings of other programs compared with those ratings of other reviewers of the same programs. The purpose of the process is to allow programmers to self-assess their programming skills. As such, the process appears to be useful in both industrial and classroom environments.

REFERENCES

1. G. M. Weinberg, *The Psychology of Computer Programming*. New York: Van Nostrand Reinhold, 1971.

2. G. J. Myers, *Software Reliability: Principles and Practices*. New York: Wiley–Interscience, 1976.

3. G. J. Myers, *Composite/Structured Design*. New York: Van Nostrand Reinhold, 1978.

4. G. J. Myers, "A Controlled Experiment in Program Testing and Code Walkthroughs/Inspections," *Commun. ACM*, 21(9), 760–768 (1978).

5. M. P. Perriens, "An Application of Formal Inspections to Top-Down Structured Program Development," RADC-TR-77-212, IBM Federal Systems Div., Gaithersburg, Md., 1977 (NTIS AD/A-041645).

6. M. L. Shooman and M. I. Bolsky, "Types, Distribution, and Test and Correction Times for Programming Errors," *Proceedings of the 1975 International Conference on Reliable Software*. New York: IEEE, 1975, pp. 347–357.

7. M. E. Fagan, "Design and Code Inspections to Reduce Errors in Program Development," *IBM Systems J.*, 15(3), 182–211 (1976).

8. R. D. Freeman, "An Experiment in Software Development," *The Bell System Technical Journal, Special Safeguard Supplement*, S199–S209 (1975).

9. J. Ascoly et al., "Code Inspection Specification," TR–21.630, IBM System Communication Division, Kingston, N.Y. 1976.

10. N. Anderson and B. Shneiderman, "Use of Peer Ratings in Evaluating Computer Program Quality," IFSM-TR-20, Unversity of Maryland, 1977.

CHAPTER 4

Test-Case Design

Apart from the psychological issues discussed in Chapter 2, the most important consideration in program testing is the design or invention of effective test cases. The reason for the importance of test-case design stems from the fact that "complete" testing is impossible and therefore a test of any program must be necessarily incomplete (i.e., the testing cannot guarantee the absence of all errors). The obvious strategy, then, is to try to reduce this incompleteness as much as possible.

Given constraints on time, cost, computer time, etc., the key issue of testing becomes

What subset of all possible test cases has the highest probability of detecting the most errors?

The study of test-case-design methodologies supplies one with answers to this question.

Probably the poorest methodology of all is random-input testing—the process of testing a program by selecting, at random, some subset of all possible input values. In terms of the probability of detecting the most errors, a randomly selected collection of test cases has little chance of being an optimal, or close to optimal, subset. What we are looking for in this chapter is a set of thought processes that allow one to select a set of test data more intelligently. Chapter 2 showed that exhaustive black-box and white-box testing are, in general, impossible, but it suggested that a reasonable testing strategy might ue elements of both. This is the strategy developed in this chapter. One can develop a reasonably rigorous test by using certain black-box-oriented test-case-design methodologies and then supplementing these test cases by examining the logic of the program (i.e., using white-box methods).

The methodologies discussed in this chapter are listed below.

Black Box	*White Box*
Equivalence partitioning	Statement coverage
Boundary-value analysis	Decision coverage
Cause–effect graphing	Condition coverage
Error guessing	Decision/condition coverage
	Multiple-condition coverage

Although the methods will be discussed separately, it is recommended that most, if not all, of the methods be used to design a rigorous test of a program, since each method has distinct strengths and weaknesses (e.g., types of errors it is likely to detect and overlook). After studying the methods, one might have reservations about this statement, since all the methods are mentally taxing, requiring a lot of hard work. One must realize, however, that program testing is inherently an extremely difficult task. To quote an old sage, "If you thought designing and coding that program was hard, you ain't seen nothing yet."

The recommended procedure is to develop test cases using the black-box methods and then develop supplementary test cases as necessary by using the white-box methods. The white-box methods, being more widely known, are discussed first.

LOGIC-COVERAGE TESTING

White-box testing is concerned with the degree to which test cases exercise or cover the logic (source code) of the program. As we saw in Chapter 2, the ultimate white-box test is the execution of every path in the program, but since in a program with loops the execution of every path is usually infeasible, complete path testing is not considered here as a viable testing goal.

If one backs completely away from path testing, it may seem

that a useful coverage criterion is to require every statement in the program to be executed at least once. Unfortunately, this is a weak criterion, so we can say that writing enough test cases such that every statement is executed at least once is a necessary, but in no way sufficient, criterion for a reasonable white-box test. This can be seen from Figure 4.1. Assume that Figure 4.1 represents a small program to be tested. The equivalent PL/I program would be

```
M:  PROCEDURE (A,B,X);
IF ( (A>1) & (B=0) ) THEN DO;
                      X=X/A;
                      END;
IF ( (A=2) I (X>1) ) THEN DO;
                      X=X+1;
                      END;
    END;
```

One could execute every statement by writing a single test case that traverses path *ace*. That is, by setting $A = 2$, $B = 0$, and $X = 3$ at point *a*, every statement would be executed once (actually, X could be assigned any value).

Unfortunately, this criterion is a rather poor one. For instance, perhaps the first decision should be an *or* rather than an *and*. If so, this error would go undetected. Perhaps the second decision should have stated X>0; this error would not be detected. Also, there is a path through the program in which X goes unchanged (the path *abd*). If this is an error, it would go undetected. In other words, the statement-coverage criterion is so weak that it is generally considered to be useless.

A stronger logic-coverage criterion is known as *decision coverage* or *branch coverage*. This criterion states that one must write enough test cases such that each decision has a *true* and *false* outcome at least once. Another way of stating it is that each branch direction must be traversed at least once. Examples of branch or decision statements or DO statements (or PERFORM UNTIL in Cobol), IF statements, and multiway GO TO statements.

Decision coverage can be shown to usually satisfy statement coverage. Since every statement is on some subpath emanating from either a branch statement or from the entry point of the program, every statement must be executed if every branch direction is executed. However, there are at least three exceptions. One is the pathological situation where the program has no deci-

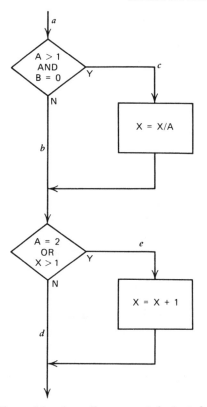

Figure 4.1   **A small program to be tested.**

sions. A second occurs in programs or subroutines with multiple
entry points; a given statement might only be executed if the
program is entered at a particular entry point. The third exception is statements within ON-units; traversing every branch direction will not necessarily cause all ON-units to be executed.
Since we have deemed statement coverage to be a necessary condition, decision coverage, a seemingly better criterion, should be
defined to include statement coverage. Hence, decision coverage
requires that each decision have a *true* and *false* outcome, *and*
that each statement be executed at least once. An alternative
and easier way of expressing it is that each decision have a *true*
and *false* outcome, and that each point of entry (including ON-
units) be invoked, at least once.

The above discussion considers only two-way decisions or
branches and has to be modified for programs containing multiway decisions. Examples are PL/I programs containing SELECT

(CASE) statements or GO-TO label-variable statements, Fortran programs containing arithmetic (three-way) IF statements or computed or arithmetic GO TO statements, and Cobol programs containing ALTERed GO TO statements or GO-TO-DEPEND-ING-ON statements. For such programs, the criterion is exercising each possible outcome of all decisions at least once and invoking each point of entry to the program or subroutine at least once.

In Figure 4.1, decision coverage can be met by two test cases covering paths ace and abd or, alternatively, acd and abe. If we choose the latter alternative, the two test-case inputs are $A = 3$, $B = 0$, $X = 3$ and $A = 2$, $B = 1$, and $X = 1$.

Decision coverage is a stronger criterion than statement coverage, but it is still rather weak. For instance, there is only a 50% chance that we would explore the path where X is not changed (i.e., only if we chose the former alternative). If the second decision was in error (e.g., if it should have said $X<1$ instead of $X>1$), the mistake would not be detected by the two test cases in the previous example.

A criterion that is sometimes stronger than decision coverage is *condition coverage*. In this case, one writes enough test cases such that each condition in a decision takes on all possible outcomes at least once. Since, as with decision coverage, this does not always lead to the execution of each statement, an addition to the criterion is that each point of entry to the program or subroutine, as well as ON-units, be invoked at least once. For instance, the branching statement

DO K=0 TO 50 WHILE (J+K<QUEST)

contains two conditions: is K less than or equal to 50, and is $J + K$ less than QUEST? Hence test cases would be required for the situations $K \leq 50$, $K > 50$ (i.e., reaching the last iteration of the loop), $J + K < $ QUEST, and $J + K \geq$ QUEST.

Figure 4.1 has four conditions: $A > 1$, $B = 0$, $A = 2$, and $X > 1$. Hence enough test cases are needed to force the situations where $A > 1$, $A \leq 1$, $B = 0$, and $B \neq 0$ are present at point a and where $A = 2$, $A \neq 2$, $X > 1$, and $X \leq 1$ at point b. A sufficient number of test cases satisfying the criterion, and the paths traversed by each, are

1. $A = 2, B = 0, X = 4$ ace
2. $A = 1, B = 1, X = 1$ adb

Note that although the same number of test cases were generated for this example, condition coverage is usually superior to decision coverage in that it *may* (but does not always) cause every individual condition in a decision to be executed with both outcomes, where decision coverage does not. For instance, the DO statement

DO K=0 TO 50 WHILE (J+K<QUEST)

is a two-way branch (execute the loop body or skip it). If one is using decision testing, the criterion can be satisfied by letting the loop run from $K = 0$ to 51, *without ever exploring the circumstance where the WHILE clause becomes false.* With the condition criterion, however, a test case would be needed that generated a *false* outcome for the condition $J + K < QUEST$.

Although the condition-coverage criterion appears, at first glance, to satisfy the decision-coverage criterion, it does not always do so. If the decision IF (A&B) is being tested, the condition-coverage criterion would allow one to write two test cases— A is *true*, B is *false*, and A is *false*, B is *true*—but this would not cause the THEN clause of the IF to execute. The condition-coverage tests for the earlier example covered all decision outcomes, but this was only by chance. For instance, two alternative test cases

1. $A = 1, B = 0, X = 3$
2. $A = 2, B = 1, X = 1$

cover all condition outcomes, but they cover only two of the four decision outcomes (they both cover path *abe* and hence do not exercise the *true* outcome of the first decision and the *false* outcome of the second decision).

The obvious way out of this dilemma is a criterion called *decision/condition coverage.* It requires sufficient test cases such that each condition in a decision takes on all possible outcomes at least once, each decision takes on all possible outcomes at least once, and each point of entry is invoked at least once.

A weakness with decision/condition coverage is that although it may appear to exercise all outcomes of all conditions, it frequently does not because certain conditions mask other conditions. To see this, examine Figure 4.2. The flowchart in Figure 4.2 is the way a compiler would generate machine code for the program in Figure 4.1. The multicondition decisions in the source program have been broken into individual decisions and branches because most machines do not have a single instruction that makes multicondition decisions. A more thorough test coverage, then, appears to be the exercising of all possible outcomes of each primitive decision. The two previous decision-coverage test cases do not accomplish this; they fail to exercise the *false* outcome of decision H and the *true* outcome of decision K. In this program, the condition-coverage test is equally deficient; the two test cases (which also happen to satisfy the decision/condition criterion) do not invoke the *false* outcome of decision I and the *true* outcome of decision K.

The reason is that, as shown in Figure 4.2, results of conditions in *and* and *or* expressions can mask or block the evaluation of other conditions. For instance, if an *and* condition is *false,* none of the subsequent conditions in the expression need be evaluated. Likewise, if an *or* condition is found to be *true,* none of the subsequent conditions need be evaluated. Hence, errors in logical expressions are not necessarily made visible by the condition-coverage and decision/condition coverage criteria.

A criterion that covers this problem, and then some, is *multiple-condition coverage.* This criterion requires one to write sufficient test cases such that all possible combinations of condition outcomes in each decision, and all points of entry, are invoked at least once. For instance, four situations to be tested exist in the following sequence of statements:

```
NOTFOUND = '1'B;
DO I=1 TO TABSIZE WHILE (NOTFOUND); /*SEARCH TABLE*/
    searching logic;
END;
```

1. I≤TABSIZE and NOTFOUND is *true.*
2. I≤TABSIZE and NOTFOUND is *false* (finding the entry before hitting the end of the table).
3. I>TABSIZE and NOTFOUND is *true* (hitting the end of the table without finding the entry).
4. I>TABSIZE and NOTFOUND is *false* (the entry is the last one in the table).

It should be easy to see that a set of test cases satisfying the multiple-condition criterion also satisfies the decision-coverage, condition-coverage, and decision/condition coverage criteria.

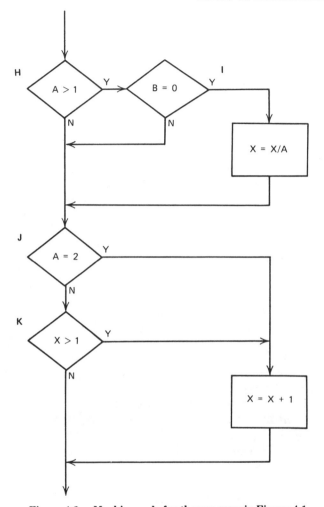

Figure 4.2 **Machine code for the program in Figure 4.1.**

Returning to Figure 4.1, eight combinations must be covered by test cases:

1. $A > 1, B = 0$ 5. $A = 2, X > 1$
2. $A > 1, B \neq 0$ 6. $A = 2, X \leq 1$
3. $A \leq 1, B = 0$ 7. $A \neq 2, X > 1$
4. $A \leq 1, B \neq 0$ 8. $A \neq 2, X \leq 1$

Note, as was the case earlier, that cases 5–8 express values at the point of the second IF statement. Since X may be altered above this IF statement, the values needed at this IF statement must be "backedup" through the logic to find the corresponding input values.

These combinations to be tested do not necessarily imply that eight test cases are needed. In fact, they can be covered by four test cases. The test-case input values, and the combinations they cover, are

$$A = 2, B = 0, X = 4 \qquad \text{covers } 1, 5$$
$$A = 2, B = 1, X = 1 \qquad \text{covers } 2, 6$$
$$A = 1, B = 0, X = 2 \qquad \text{covers } 3, 7$$
$$A = 1, B = 1, X = 1 \qquad \text{covers } 4, 8$$

The fact that there are four test cases and that there are four distinct paths in Figure 4.1 is just coincidence. In fact, the above four tests cases do not cover every path; they miss the path acd. For instance, eight test cases would be needed for the following program:

```
IF ((X=Y) & (LENGTH(Z)=0) & END) THEN J=1;
                               ELSE  I=1;
```

although it contains only two paths. In the case of loops, the number of test cases required by the multiple-condition criterion is normally much less than the number of paths.

In summary, for programs containing only one condition per decision, a minimum test criterion is a sufficient number of test cases to (1) evoke all outcomes of each decision at least once and (2) invoke each point of entry (e.g., entry point, ON-unit) at least once (to ensure that all statements are executed at least once). For programs containing decisions having multiple conditions, the minimum criterion is a sufficient number of test cases to evoke all possible combinations of condition outcomes in each decision, and all points of entry to the program, at least once. [The word "possible" is inserted because some combinations may be found to be impossible to create; for instance, only three combinations of conditions in the decision $(A>2)\&(A<10)$ can be created.]

EQUIVALENCE PARTITIONING

Chapter 2 described a good test case as one that has a reasonable probability of finding an error, and it also discussed the fact that an exhaustive-input test of a program is impossible. Hence, in testing a program, one is limited to trying a small subset of all possible inputs. Of course, then, one wants to select the right subset (i.e., the subset with the highest probability of finding the most errors).

One way of locating this subset is to realize that a well-selected test case should also have two other properties:

1. It reduces, by more than a count of one, the number of other test cases tht must be developed to achieve some predefined goal of "reasonable" testing.
2. It covers a large set of other possible test cases. That is, it tells us something about the presence or absence of errors over and above this specific set of input values.

These two properties, although they appear to be similar, describe two distinct considerations. The first implies that each test case should invoke as many different input conditions as possible in order to minimize the total number of test cases necessary. The second implies that one should try to partition the input domain of a program into a finite number of *equivalence classes* such that one can reasonably assume (but, of course, not be absolutely sure) that a test of a representative value of each class is equivalent to a test of any other value. That is, if one test case in an equivalence class detects an error, all other test cases in the equivalence class would be expected to find the same error. Conversely, if a test case did not detect an error, we would expect that no other test cases in the equivalence class would find an error (unless a subset of the equivalence class falls within another equivalence class, since equivalence classes may overlap one another).

These two considerations form a black-box methodology known as *equivalence partitioning*. The second consideration is used to develop a set of "interesting" conditions to be tested. The first consideration is then used to develop a minimal set of test cases covering these conditions.

An example of an equivalence class in the triangle program of Chapter 1 is the set "three equal-valued numbers having integer values greater than zero." By identifying this as an equivalence class, we are stating that if no error is found by a test of one element of the set, it is unlikely that an error would be found by a test of another element of the set. In other words, our testing time is best spent elsewhere (in different equivalence classes).

Test-case design by equivalence partitioning proceeds in two steps: (1) identifying the equivalence classes and (2) defining the test cases.

Identifying the Equivalence Classes

The equivalence classes are identified by taking each input condition (usually a sentence or phrase in the specification) and partitioning it into two or more groups. In doing this, the table in Figure 4.3 is used. Notice that two types of equivalence classes are identified: *valid equivalence classes* represent valid inputs to the program, and *invalid equivalence classes* represent all other possible states of the condition (i.e., erroneous input values). Thus we are adhering to the principle discussed in Chapter 2 that stated that one must focus attention on invalid or unexpected conditions.

Given an input or external condition, identifying the equivalence classes is largely a heuristic process. A set of guidelines is

1. If an input condition specifies a *range* of values (e.g., "the item count can be from 1 to 999"), identify one valid equivalence class (1<item count<999) and two invalid equivalence classes (item count<1 and item count>999).
2. If an input condition specifies the *number* of values (e.g., "one through six owners can be listed for the automobile"), identify one valid equivalence class and two invalid equivalence classes (no owners and more than six owners).

External condition	Valid equivalence classes	Invalid equivalence classes

Figure 4.3   A form for enumerating equivalence classes.

3. If an input condition specifies a *set* of input values and there is reason to believe that each is handled differently by the program (e.g., "type of vehicle must be BUS, TRUCK, TAXI-CAB, PASSENGER, or MOTORCYCLE"), identify a valid equivalence class for each and one invalid equivalence class (e.g., "TRAILER").

4. If an input condition specifies a "must be" situation (e.g., "first character of the identifier must be a letter"), identify one valid equivalence class (it is a letter) and one invalid equivalence class (it is not a letter).

5. If there is any reason to believe that elements in an equivalence class are not handled in an identical manner by the program, split the equivalence class into smaller equivalence classes.

An example of this process will be illustrated shortly.

Identifying the Test Cases

The second step is the use of equivalence classes to identify the test cases. The process is

1. Assign a unique number to each equivalence class.
2. Until all valid equivalence classes have been covered by (incorporated into) test cases, write a new test case covering as many of the uncovered valid equivalence classes as possible.
3. Until all invalid equivalence classes have been covered by test cases, write a test case that covers one, and only one, of the uncovered invalid equivalence classes.

The reason that invalid cases are covered by individual test cases is that certain erroneous-input checks mask or supersede other erroneous-input checks. For instance, if the specification states "enter book type (HARDCOVER, SOFTCOVER, or LOOSE) and amount (1–9999)," the test case

    XYZ   0

expressing two error conditions (invalid book type and amount) will probably not exercise the check for the amount, since the program may say "XYZ IS UNKNOWN BOOK TYPE" and not bother to examine the remainder of the input.

An Example

As an example, assume that we are developing a compiler for a subset of the Fortran language and we wish to test the syntax checking of the DIMENSION statement. The specification is listed below. (This is not the full Fortran DIMENSION statement; it has been cut down considerably to make it a "textbook-sized" example. Do not be deluded into thinking that the testing of actual programs is as easy as the examples in this book.) In the specification, items in italics indicate syntactic units for which specific entities must be substituted in actual statements, brackets are used to indicate optional items, and an ellipsis indicates that the preceding item may appear multiple times in succession.

A DIMENSION statement is used to specify the dimensions of arrays. The form of the DIMENSION statement is
  DIMENSION *ad*[,*ad*]...
where *ad* is an array descriptor of the form
  n (*d*[,*d*]...)
where *n* is the symbolic name of the array and *d* is a dimension declarator. Symbolic names can be one–six letters or digits, the first of which must be a letter. The minimum and maximum numbers of dimension declarations that can be specified for an array are one and seven, respectively. The form of a dimension declarator is
  [*lb*:]*ub*
where *lb* and *ub* are the lower and upper dimension bounds. A bound may be a constant in the range -65534 to 65535 or the name of an integer variable (but not an array element name). If *lb* is not specified, it is assumed to be one. The value of *ub* must be greater than or equal to *lb*. If *lb* is specified, its value may be negative, zero, or positive. As for all statements, the DIMENSION statement may be continued over multiple lines. (End of specification.)

The first step is to identify the input conditions and, from these, locate the equivalence classes. These are tabulated in Table 4.1. The numbers in the table are unique identifiers of the equivalence classes.

The next step is to write a test case covering one or more valid equivalence classes. For instance, the test case

DIMENSION A (2)

covers classes 1, 4, 7, 10, 12, 15, 24, 28, 29, and 40. The next step is

Table 4.1   Equivalence Classes

Input condition	Valid equivalence classes	Invalid equivalence classes
No. of array descriptors	one (1), >one (2)	none (3)
Size of array name	1–6 (4)	0 (5), >6 (6)
Array name	has letters (7), has digits (8)	has something else (9)
Array name starts with letter	yes (10)	no (11)
No. of dimensions	1–7 (12)	0 (13), >7 (14)
Upper bound is	constant (15), integer variable (16)	array element name (17), something else (18)
Integer variable name	has letters (19), has digits (20)	has something else (21)
Integer variable starts with letter	yes (22)	no (23)
Constant	−65534–65535 (24)	<−65534 (25), >65535 (26)
Lower bound specified	yes (27), no (28)	
Upper bound to lower bound	greater than (29), equal (30)	less than (31)
Specified lower bound	negative (32), zero (33), >0 (34)	
Lower bound is	constant (35), integer variable (36)	array element name (37), something else (38)
Multiple lines	yes (39), no (40)	

to devise one or more test cases covering the remaining valid equivalence classes. One test case of the form

```
      DIMENSION A12345 (I,9,J4XXXX,65535,1,KLM,
  X     100), BBB(−65534:100,0:1000,10:10, I:65535)
```

covers the remaining classes. The invalid-input equivalence classes, and a test case representing each, are

   (3):   DIMENSION
   (5):   DIMENSION (10)
   (6):   DIMENSION A234567(2)
   (9):   DIMENSION A. 1(2)
 (11):   DIMENSION 1A (10)

```
(13):   DIMENSION B
(14):   DIMENSION B (4,4,4,4,4,4,4,4)
(17):   DIMENSION B (4,A(2))
(18):   DIMENSION B (4,,7)
(21):   DIMENSION C (I.,10)
(23):   DIMENSION C (10,1J)
(25):   DIMENSION D (-65535:1)
(26):   DIMENSION D (65536)
(31):   DIMENSION D (4:3)
(37):   DIMENSION D (A(2):4)
(38):   DIMENSION D (.:4)
```

Hence the equivalence classes have been covered by 18 test cases. The reader may want to consider how these test cases would compare to a set of test cases derived in an ad hoc manner.

Although equivalence partitioning is vastly superior to a random selection of test cases, it still has deficiencies (i.e., it overlooks certain types of high-yield test cases). The next two methodologies, boundary-value analysis and cause-effect graphing, cover many of these deficiencies.

BOUNDARY-VALUE ANALYSIS

Experience shows that test cases that explore *boundary conditions* have a higher payoff than test cases that do not. Boundary conditions are those situations directly on, above, and beneath the edges of input equivalence classes and output equivalence classes. Boundary-value analysis differs from equivalence partitioning in two respects

1. Rather than selecting *any* element in an equivalence class as being representative, boundary-value analysis requires that one or more elements be selected such that each edge of the equivalence class is the subject of a test.
2. Rather than just focusing attention on the input conditions (input space), test cases are also derived by considering the *result space* (i.e., output equivalence classes).

It is difficult to present a "cookbook" for boundary-value analysis, since it requires a degree of creativity and a certain amount of specialization toward the problem at hand. (Hence, like many other aspects of testing, it is more a state of mind than anything else.) However, a few general guidelines are

1. If an input condition specifies a range of values, write test cases for the ends of the range, and invalid-input test cases for situations just beyond the ends. For instance, if the valid domain of an input value is $-1.0-+1.0$, write test cases for the situations $-1.0, 1.0, -1.001$, and 1.001.
2. If an input condition specifies a number of values, write test cases for the minimum and maximum number of values and one beneath and beyond these values. For instance, if an input file can contain 1–255 records, write test cases for 0, 1, 255, and 256 records.
3. Use guideline 1 for each output condition. For instance, if a program computes the monthly FICA deduction and if the minimum is $0.00 and the maximum is $1165.25, write test cases that cause $0.00 and $1165.25 to be deducted. Also, see if it is possible to invent test cases that might cause a negative deduction or a deduction of more than $1165.25. Note that it is important to examine the boundaries of the result space because it is not always the case that the boundaries of the input domains represent the same set of circumstances as the boundaries of the output ranges (e.g., consider a sine subroutine). Also, it is not always possible to generate a result outside of the output range, but it is worth considering the possibility, none the less.
4. Use guideline 2 for each output condition. If an information-retrieval system displays the most-relevant abstracts based on an input request, but never more than four abstracts, write test cases such that the program displays zero, one, and four abstracts, and write a test case that might cause the program to erroneously display five abstracts.
5. If the input or output of a program is an ordered set (e.g., a sequential file, linear list, table), focus attention on the first and last elements of the set.
6. In addition, use your ingenuity to search for other boundary conditions.

The triangle-analysis program of Chapter 1 can be used to illustrate the need for boundary-value analysis. For the input values to represent a triangle, they must be integers greater than 0 where the sum of any two is greater than the third. If one was defining equivalence partitions, one might define one where this condition is met, and another where the sum of two of the integers is not greater than the third. Hence two possible test cases might be 3–4–5 and 1–2–4. However, we have missed a likely error. That is, if an expression in the program was coded as A+B≥C instead of A+B>C, the program would erroneously tell us that 1–2–3 represents a valid scalene triangle. Hence the important difference between boundary-value analysis and equivalence partitioning is that boundary-value analysis explores situations *on and around the edges of the equivalence partitions.*

As an example of a boundary-value analysis, consider the following program specification.

MTEST is a program that grades multiple-choice examinations. The input is a file named OCR, which contains 80-character records. The first record is a title; the contents of this record are used as a title on each output report. The next set of records describes the correct answers on the exam. Each record contains a "2" as the last character. In the first record of this set, the number of questions is listed in columns 1–3 (a value of 1–999). Columns 10–59 contain the correct answers for questions 1–50 (any character is valid as an answer). Subsequent record contain, in columns 10–59, the correct answers for questions 51–100, 101–150, and so on.

The third set of records describes the answers of each student; each record contains a "3" in column 80. For each student, the first record contains the student's name or number in columns 1–9 (any characters); columns 10–59 contain the student's answers for questions 1–50. If the test has more than 50 questions, subsequent records for the student contain answers 51–100, 101–150, and so on, in columns 10–59. The maximum number of students is 200. The input data are illustrated in Figure 4.4

The four output records are (1) a report, sorted by student identifier, showing each student's grade (percentage of answers correct) and rank; (2) a similar report, but sorted by grade; (3) a report indicating the mean, median, and standard deviation of the grades; and (4) a report, ordered by question number, showing the percentage of students answering each question correctly. (End of specification.)

We can begin by methodically reading the specification, looking for input conditions. The first boundary input condition is an empty input file. The second input condition is the title card;

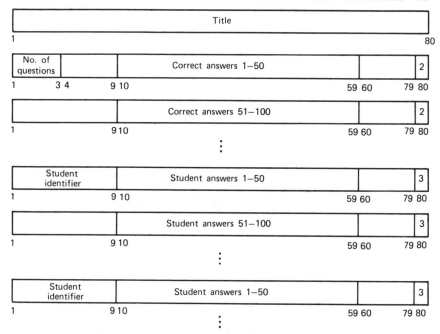

Figure 4.4   **Inpur to the MTEST program.**

boundary conditions are a missing title card and shortest and longest possible titles. The next input conditions are the presence of correct-answer records and the number-of-questions field on the first answer record. The equivalence class for the number of questions is not 1–999, since something special happens at each multiple of 50 (i.e., multiple records are needed). A reasonable partitioning of this into equivalence classes is 1-50 and 51-999. Hence we need test cases where the number-of-questions field is set to 0, 1, 50, 51, and 999. This covers most of the boundary conditions for the number of correct-answer records; however, three more interesting situations are the absence of answer records and having one-too-many and one-too-few answer records (e.g., the number of questions is 60, but there are three answer records in one case and one answer record in the other case). The test cases identified so far are

1. Empty input file
2. Missing title record
3. 1-character title

  4.   80-character title
  5.   1-question exam
  6.   50-question exam
  7.   51-question exam
  8.   999-question exam
  9.   0-question exam
 10.   Number-of-questions field has nonnumeric value.
 11.   No correct-answer records after title record
 12.   One too many correct-answer records
 13.   One too few correct-answer records

The next input conditions are related to the students' answers. The boundary-value test cases here appear to be

 14.   0 students
 15.   1 student
 16.   200 students
 17.   201 students
 18.   A student has one answer record, but there are two correct-answer records.
 19.   The above student is the first student in the file.
 20.   The above student is the last student in the file.
 21.   A student has two answer records, but there is just one correct-answer record.
 22.   The above student is the first student in the file.
 23.   The above student is the last student in the file.

One can also derive a useful set of test cases by examining the output boundaries, although some of the output boundaries (e.g., empty report 1) are covered by the existing test cases. The boundary conditions of reports 1 and 2 are

   0 students (same as test 14)
   1 student (same as test 15)
   200 students (same as test 16)
 24.   All students receive the same grade.
 25.   All students receive a different grade.
 26.   Some, but not all, students receive the same grade (to see if ranks are computed correctly).
 27.   A student receives a grade of 0.
 28.   A student receives a grade of 100.
 29.   A student has the lowest possible identifier value (to check the sort).

30. A student has the highest possible identifier value.
31. The number of students is such that the report is just large enough to fit on one page (to see if an extraneous page is printed).
32. The number of students is such that all students but one fit on one page.

The boundary conditions from report 3 (mean, median, and standard deviation) are

33. The mean is at its maximum (all students have a perfect score).
34. The mean is 0 (all students receive a grade of 0).
35. The standard deviation is at its maximum (one student receives a 0 and the other receives a 100).
36. The standard deviation is 0 (all students receive the same grade).

Tests 33 and 34 also cover the boundaries of the median. Another useful test case is the situation where there are 0 students (looking for a division by 0 in computing the mean), but this is identical to test case 14.

An examination of report 4 yields the following boundary-value tests:

37. All students answer question 1 correctly.
38. All students answer question 1 incorrectly.
39. All students answer the last question correctly.
40. All students answer the last question incorrectly.
41. The number of questions is such that the report is just large enough to fit on one page.
42. The number of questions is such that all questions but one fit on one page.

An experienced programmer would probably agree at this point that many of these 42 test cases represent common errors that might have been made in developing this program, yet most of these errors would probably go undetected if a random or ad hoc test-case-generation method was used. Boundary-value analysis, if practiced correctly, is one of the most useful test-case-design methods. However, it is often used ineffectively because the technique, on the surface, sounds simple. The reader should understand that boundary conditions may be very subtle and, hence, identification of them requires a lot of thought.

CAUSE–EFFECT GRAPHING

One weakness of boundary-value analysis and equivalence partitioning is that they do not explore *combinations* of input circumstances. For instance, perhaps the MTEST program of the previous section fails if the product of the number of questions and the number of students exceeds some limit (e.g., the program runs out of storage). Such an error would not necessarily be detected by boundary-value testing.

The testing of input combinations is not a simple task, because, even if one equivalence-partitions the input conditions, the number of combinations is usually astronomical. If one has no systematic way of selecting a subset of input conditions, an arbitrary subset is usually selected, leading to an inefficient test.

Cause–effect graphing [1] is a technique that aids in selecting, in a systematic way, a high-yield set of test cases. It has a beneficial side effect in pointing out incompleteness and ambiguities in the specification.

A cause–effect graph is a formal language into which a natural-language specification is translated. The graph is actually a digital-logic circuit (a combinatorial logic network), but rather than using standard electronics notation, a somewhat simpler notation is used. No knowledge of electronics is necessary other than an understanding of Boolean logic (i.e., understanding the logic operators *and, or,* and *not*).

The following process is used to derive test cases:

1. The specification is divided into "workable" pieces. This is necessary because cause–effect graphing becomes unwieldy when used on large specifications. For instance, when testing a time-sharing system, a "workable piece" might be the specification for an individual command. When testing a compiler, one might treat each programming-language statement individually.
2. The causes and effects in the specification are identified. A *cause* is a distinct input condition or an equivalence class of input conditions. An *effect* is an output condition or a system transformation (a lingering effect that an input has on the state of the program or system). For instance, if a transaction to a program causes a master file to be updated, the alteration to the master file is a system transformation; a confirmation message would be an output condition. Causes and effects are identified by reading the specification word by

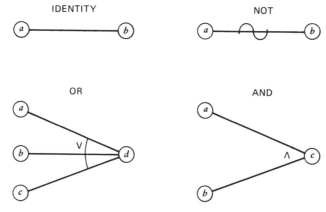

Figure 4.5   **Basic cause–effect graph symbols.**

word and underlining words or phrases that describe causes and effects. Each cause and effect is assigned an unique number.

3.   The semantic content of the specification is analyzed and transformed into a Boolean graph linking the causes and effects. This is the cause–effect graph.

4.   The graph is annotated with constraints describing combinations of causes and/or effects that are impossible because of syntactic or environmental constraints.

5.   By methodically tracing state conditions in the graph, the graph is converted into a limited-entry decision table. Each column in the table represents a test case.

6.   The columns in the decision table are converted into test cases.

The basic notation for the graph is shown in Figure 4.5. Think of each node as having the value 0 or 1; 0 represents the "absent" state and 1 represents the "present" state. The *identity* function states that if a is 1, b is 1; else b is 0. The *not* function states that if a is 1, b is 0; else b is 1. The *or* function states that if a or b or c is 1, d is 1; else d is 0. The *and* function states that if both a and b are 1, c is 1; else c is 0. The latter two functions are allowed to have any number of inputs.

To illustrate a small graph, consider the following specification.

The character in column 1 must be an "A" or a "B." The character in column 2 must be a digit. In this situation, the file update is made. If the first character is incorrect, message X12 is issued. If the second character is not a digit, message X13 is issued.

The causes are

1—character in column 1 is "A"
2—character in column 1 is "B"
3—character in column 2 is a digit

and the effects are

70—update made
71—message X12 is issued
72—message X13 is issued

The cause–effect graph is shown in Figure 4.6. Notice the intermediate node 11 that was created. The reader should confirm that the graph represents the specification by setting all possible states of the causes and seeing that the effects are set to the correct values. For readers familiar with logic diagrams, Figure 4.7 is the equivalent logic circuit.

Although the graph in Figure 4.6 represents the specification, it does contain an impossible combination of causes—it is impossible for both causes 1 and 2 to be set to 1 simultaneously. In most

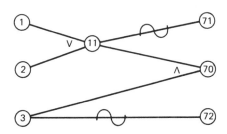

Figure 4.6   Sample cause–effect graph.

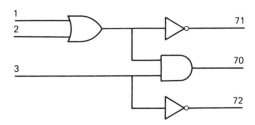

Figure 4.7   Logic–diagram equivalent to Figure 4.6.

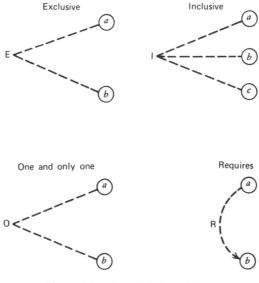

Figure 4.8   Constraint symbols.

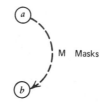

Figure 4.9   Symbol for "masks" constraint.

programs, certain combinations of causes are impossible because of syntactic or environmental considerations (e.g., a character cannot be an "A" and a "B" simultaneously). To account for these, the notation in Figure 4.8 is used. The E constraint states that it must always be true that at most one of a and b can be 1 (a and b cannot be 1 simultaneously). The I constraint states that at least one of a, b, and c must always be 1 (a, b, and c cannot be 0 simultaneously). The O constraint states that one, and only one, of a and b must be 1. The R constraint states that, for a to be 1, b must be 1 (i.e., it is impossible for a to be 1 and b to be 0).

There is frequently a need for a constraint among effects. The M constraint in Figure 4.9 states that if effect a is 1, effect b is forced to 0.

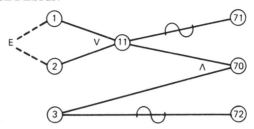

Figure 4.10   Sample cause–effect graph with "exclusive" constraint.

Returning to the simple example above, we see that it is physically impossible for causes 1 and 2 to be present simultaneously, but it is possible for neither to be present. Hence they are linked with the *E* constraint as shown in Figure 4.10.

To illustrate how cause–effect graphing is used to derive test cases, the specification in the following paragraphs will be used. The specification is for a debugging command in an interactive system.

The DISPLAY command is used to view, from a terminal, the contents of storage locations. The command syntax is shown in Figure 4.11. Brackets represent alternative optional operands. Capital letters represent operand keywords; lower-case letters represent operand values (i.e., actual values are to be substituted). Underlined operands represent the default values (i.e., the value used when the operand is omitted).

The first operand (*hexloc1*) specifies the address of the first byte whose contents are to be displayed. The address may be 1–6 hexadecimal digits (0–9, A–F) in length. If it is not specified, the address 0 is assumed. The address must be within the actual storage range of the machine.

The second operand specifies the amount of storage to be displayed. If *hexloc2* is specified, it defines the address of the last byte in a range of locations to be displayed. It may be 1–6 hexadecimal digits in length. This address must be greater than or equal to the starting address (*hexloc1*). Also, *hexloc2* must be within the actual storage range of the machine. If END is specified, storage is displayed up through the last actual byte in the machine. If *bytecount* is specified, it defines the number the number of bytes of storage to be displayed (starting with the one at *hexloc1*). The operand *bytecount* is a hexadecimal integer (one to six digits). The sum of *bytecount* and *hexloc1* must not exceed the actual storage size plus 1, and *bytecount* must have a value of at least 1.

Figure 4.11   Syntax of the DISPLAY command.

When storage is displayed, the output format on the terminal screen is one or more lines of the format

$$xxxxxx = word1\ word2\ word3\ word4$$

where $xxxxxx$ is the hexadecimal address of *word1*. An integral number of words (four-byte sequences, where the address of the first byte in the word is a multiple of four) is always displayed, regardless of the value of *hexloc1* or the amount of storage to be displayed. All output lines will always contain four words (16 bytes). The first byte of the displayed range will fall within the first word.

The error messages that can be produced are

M1 INVALID COMMAND SYNTAX
M2 STORAGE REQUESTED IS BEYOND ACTUAL STORAGE LIMIT
M3 STORAGE REQUESTED IS A ZERO OR NEGATIVE RANGE

As examples,

DISPLAY

displays the first four words in storage (default starting address of 0, default byte count of 1),

DISPLAY 77F

displays the word containing the byte at address 77F and the three subsequent words,

DISPLAY 77F-407A

displays the words containing the bytes in the address range 77F–407A,

DISPLAY 77F.6

displays the words containing the six bytes starting at location 77F, and

DISPLAY 50FF-END

displays the words containing the bytes in the address range 50FF to the end of storage.

The first step is a careful analysis of the specification to identify the causes and effects. The causes are

1. First operand is present.
2. The *hexloc1* operand contains only hexadecimal digits.
3. The *hexloc1* operand contains 1–6 characters.
4. The *hexloc1* operand is within the actual storage range.
5. Second operand is END.
6. Second operand is *hexloc2*.
7. Second operand is *bytecount*.
8. Second operand is omitted.
9. The *hexloc2* operand contains only hexadecimal digits.
10. The *hexloc2* operand contains 1–6 characters.
11. The *hexloc2* operand is within the actual storage range.
12. The *hexloc2* operand is greater than or equal to the *hexloc1* operand.
13. The *bytecount* operand contains only hexadecimal digits.
14. The *bytecount* operand contains 1–6 characters.
15. $bytecount + hexloc1 \leq$ storage size $+ 1$
16. $bytecount \geq 1$
17. Specified range is large enough to require multiple output lines.
18. Start of range does not fall on a word boundary.

Each cause has been given an arbitrary unique number. Notice that four causes (5–8) are necessary for the second operand because the second operand could be (1) END, (2) *hexloc2*, (3) *bytecount*, (4) absent, and (5) none of the above. The effects are

91. Message M1 is displayed.
92. Message M2 is displayed.
93. Message M3 is displayed.
94. Storage is displayed on one line.
95. Storage is displayed on multiple lines.
96. First byte of displayed range falls on word boundary.
97. First byte of displayed range does not fall on word boundary.

The next step is the development of the graph. The cause nodes are listed vertically on the left side of a sheet of paper; the effect nodes are listed vertically on the right side. The semantic

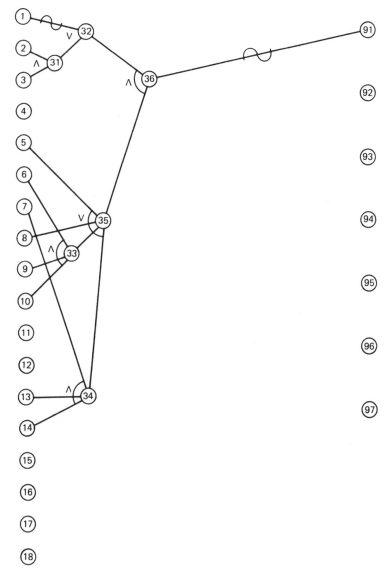

Figure 4.12   **Beginning the graph for the DISPLAY command.**

content of the specification is carefully analyzed to interconnect
the causes and effects (i.e., to show under what conditions an
effect is present).

Figure 4.12 shows an initial version of the graph. Intermediate node 32 represents a syntactically valid first operand; node 35

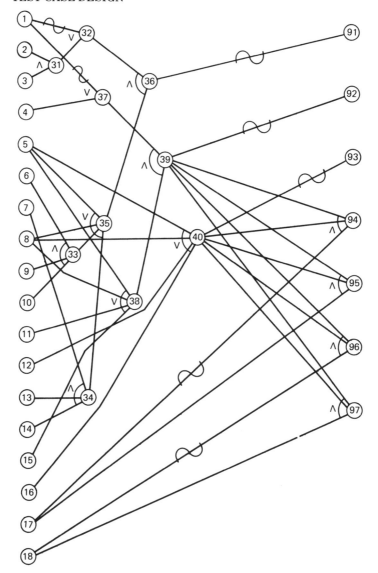

Figure 4.13   **Full cause–effect graph without constraints.**

represents a syntactically valid second operand. Node 36 represents a syntactically valid command. If node 36 is a 1, effect 91
(the error message) does not appear. If node 36 is a 0, effect 91 is
present.

   The full graph is shown in Figure 4.13. The reader should

explore the graph carefully to convince himself that it accurately reflects the specification.

If Figure 4.13 were used to derive the test cases, many impossible-to-create test cases would be derived. The reason is that certain combinations of causes are impossible because of syntactic constraints. For instance, causes 2 and 3 cannot be present unless cause 1 is present. Cause 4 cannot be present unless both causes 2 and 3 are present. Figure 4.14 contains the complete graph with the constraint conditions. Notice that at most one of causes 5, 6, 7, and 8 can be present. All other cause constraints are the *requires* condition. Notice that cause 17 (multiple output lines) requires the *not* of cause 8 (second operand is omitted); cause 17 can only be present when cause 8 is absent. Again, the reader should explore the constraint conditions carefully.

The next step is the generation of a limited-entry decision table. For readers familiar with decision tables, the causes are the conditions and the effects are the actions. The procedure that is used is

1.   Select an effect to be in the present (1) state.
2.   Tracing back through the graph, find all combinations of causes (subject to the constraints) that will set this effect to 1.
3.   Create a column in the decision table for each combination of causes.
4.   For each combination, determine the states of all other effects and place these in each column.

In performing step two, two considerations are

1.   When tracing back through an *or* node whose output should be 1, never set more than one input to the *or* to 1 simultaneously. This is called *path sensitizing*. Its objective is to avoid not detecting certain errors because of one cause masking another cause.
2.   When tracing back through an *and* node whose output should be 0, all combinations of inputs leading to a 0 output must, of course, be enumerated. However, if one is exploring the situation where one input is 0 and one or more of the others are 1, it is not necessary to enumerate all conditions under which the other inputs can be 1.
3.   When tracing back through an *and* node whose output should be 0, only one condition where *all* inputs are zero need be enumerated. (If the *and* is in the middle of the graph such

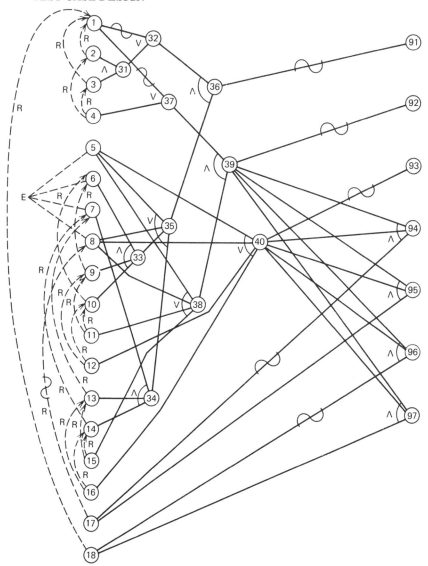

Figure 4.14   Complete cause–effect graph of the DISPLAY command.

that its inputs come from other intermediate nodes, there may be an excessively large number of situations under which all of its inputs are 0.)

These complicated considerations are summarized in Figure

Situation   States

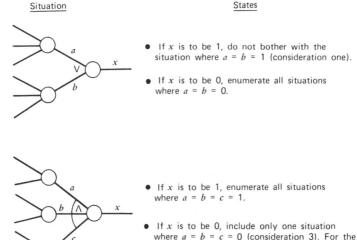

- If x is to be 1, do not bother with the situation where $a = b = 1$ (consideration one).

- If x is to be 0, enumerate all situations where $a = b = 0$.

- If x is to be 1, enumerate all situations where $a = b = c = 1$.

- If x is to be 0, include only one situation where $a = b = c = 0$ (consideration 3). For the states 001, 010, 100, 011, 101, and 110 of a, b, and c, include only one situation each (consideration 2).

Figure 4.15   **Considerations used when tracing the graph.**

4.15. Figure 4.16 is used as an example. Assume that we wish to locate all input conditions that cause the output state to be 0. Consideration 3 states that we should list only one circumstance where nodes 5 and 6 are zero. Consideration 2 states that, for the state where node 5 is 1 and node 6 is 0, we should list only one circumstance where node 5 is 1, rather than enumerating all possible ways that node 5 can be 1. Likewise, for the state where node 5 is 0 and node 6 is 1, we should list only one circumstance where node 6 is 1 (although there is only one in this example). Consideration 1 states that where node 5 should be set to 1, we should not set nodes 1 and 2 to 1 simultaneously. Hence we would arrive at five states of nodes 1–4, for example, the values

$$
\begin{array}{cccc}
0 \ \ 0 \ \ 0 \ \ 0 & (5{=}0, 6{=}0) \\
1 \ \ 0 \ \ 0 \ \ 0 & (5{=}1, 6{=}0) \\
1 \ \ 0 \ \ 0 \ \ 1 & (5{=}1, 6{=}0) \\
1 \ \ 0 \ \ 1 \ \ 0 & (5{=}1, 6{=}0) \\
0 \ \ 0 \ \ 1 \ \ 1 & (5{=}0, 6{=}1)
\end{array}
$$

rather than the 13 possible states of nodes 1–4 that lead to a 0 output state.

These considerations may appear to be capricious, but they have an important purpose: to lessen the combinatorics of the

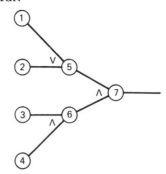

Figure 4.16 Sample graph to illustrate the tracing considerations.

graph. They eliminate situations that tend to be low-yield test cases. If low-yield test cases are not eliminated, a large cause–effect graph will produce an astronomical number of test cases. If the number of test cases is too large to be practical, one will select some subset, but there is no guarantee that the low-yield test cases will be the ones eliminated. Hence it is better to eliminate them during the analysis of the graph.

The cause–effect graph in Figure 4.14 will now be converted into the decision table. Effect 91 will be selected first. Effect 91 is present if node 36 is 0. Node 36 is 0 if nodes 32 and 35 are 0,0 0,1, or 1,0, and considerations 2 and 3 apply here. By tracing back to the causes and considering the constraints among causes, one can find the combinations of causes that lead to effect 91 being present, although doing so is a laborious process.

The resultant decision table under the condition that effect 91 is present is shown in Figure 4.17 (columns 1–11). Columns (tests) 1–3 represent the conditions where node 32 is 0 and node 35 is 1. Columns 4–10 represent the conditions where node 32 is 1 and node 35 is 0. Using consideration 3, only one situation (column 11) out of a possible 21 situations where nodes 32 and 35 are 0 is identified. Blanks in the table represent "don't care" situations (i.e., the state of the cause is irrelevant) or indicate that the state of a cause is obvious because of the states of other dependent causes (e.g., in column 1, we know that causes 5, 7, and 8 must be 0 because they exist in an "at most one" situation with cause 6).

Columns 12–15 represent the situations where effect 92 is present. Columns 16 and 17 represent the situations where effect 93 is present. Figure 4.18 represents the remainder of the decision table.

The last step is to convert the decision table into 38 test cases.

A set of 38 test cases is listed below. The number or numbers beside each test case designate the effects that are expected to be present. Assume that the last location in storage on the machine being used is 7FFF.

1.	DISPLAY 234AF74-123	(91)
2.	DISPLAY 2ZX4-3000	(91)
3.	DISPLAY HHHHHHHH-2000	(91)
4.	DISPLAY 200 200	(91)
5.	DISPLAY 0-22222222	(91)
6.	DISPLAY 1-2X	(91)
7.	DISPLAY 2-ABCDEFGHI	(91)
8.	DISPLAY 3.1111111	(91)
9.	DISPLAY 44.$42	(91)
10.	DISPLAY 100.$$$$$$$	(91)
11.	DISPLAY 10000000-M	(91)
12.	DISPLAY FF-8000	(92)
13.	DISPLAY FFF.7001	(92)
14.	DISPLAY 8000-END	(92)
15.	DISPLAY 8000-8001	(92)
16.	DISPLAY AA-A9	(93)
17.	DISPLAY 7000.0	(93)
18.	DISPLAY 7FF9-END	(94, 97)
19.	DISPLAY 1	(94, 97)
20.	DISPLAY 21-29	(94, 97)
21.	DISPLAY 4021.A	(94, 97)
22.	DISPLAY-END	(94, 96)
23.	DISPLAY	(94, 96)
24.	DISPLAY-F	(94, 96)
25.	DISPLAY .E	(94, 96)
26.	DISPLAY 7FF8-END	(94, 96)
27.	DISPLAY 6000	(94, 96)
28.	DISPLAY A0-A4	(94, 96)
29.	DISPLAY 20.8	(94, 96)
30.	DISPLAY 7001-END	(95, 97)
31.	DISPLAY 5-15	(95, 97)
32.	DISPLAY 4FF.100	(95, 97)
33.	DISPLAY -END	(95, 96)
34.	DISPLAY -20	(95, 96)
35.	DISPLAY .11	(95, 96)
36.	DISPLAY 7000-END	(95, 96)
37.	DISPLAY 4-14	(95, 96)
38.	DISPLAY 500.11	(95, 96)

	1	2	3	4	5	6	7	8	9	10	11	12	13	14	15	16	17
1	1	1	1	1	1	1	1	1	1	1	1	1	1	1	1	1	1
2	1	0	0	1	1	1	1	1	1	1	1	1	1	1	1	1	1
3	0	1	0	1	1	1	1	1	1	1	0	1	1	1	1	1	1
4												1	1	0	0	1	1
5				0										1			
6	1	1	1	0	1	1	1					1	1		1	1	
7				0			1	1	1				1				1
8				0													
9	1	1	1		1	0	0				0	1			1	1	
10	1	1	1		0	1	0				1	1			1	1	
11													0		0	1	
12																0	
13							1	0	0				1				1
14							0	1	0				1				1
15													0				
16																	0
17																	
18																	
91	1	1	1	1	1	1	1	1	1	1	1	1	0	0	0	0	0
92	0	0	0	0	0	0	0	0	0	0	0	0	1	1	1	1	0
93	0	0	0	0	0	0	0	0	0	0	0	0	0	0	0	1	1
94	0	0	0	0	0	0	0	0	0	0	0	0	0	0	0	0	0
95	0	0	0	0	0	0	0	0	0	0	0	0	0	0	0	0	0
96	0	0	0	0	0	0	0	0	0	0	0	0	0	0	0	0	0
97	0	0	0	0	0	0	0	0	0	0	0	0	0	0	0	0	0

Figure 4.17   **First half of the resultant decision table.**

Note that where two or more different test cases invoked, for the most part, the same set of causes, different values for the causes were selected to slightly improve the yield of the test cases. Also note that, because of the actual storage size, test case 22 is impossible (it will yield effect 95 instead of 94, as noted in test case 33). Hence 37 test cases have been identified.

Remarks

Cause–effect graphing is a systematic method of generating test cases representing combinations of conditions. The alternative would be an ad hoc selection of combinations, but, in doing

	18	19	20	21	22	23	24	25	26	27	28	29	30	31	32	33	34	35	36	37	38
1	1	1	1	1	0	0	0	0	1	1	1	1	1	1	1	1	0	0	1	1	1
2	1	1	1	1					1	1	1	1	1	1	1	1			1	1	1
3	1	1	1	1					1	1	1	1	1	1	1	1			1	1	1
4	1	1	1	1					1	1	1	1	1	1	1	1			1	1	1
5	1			1					1				1			1		1			
6		1				1					1			1			1			1	
7			1				1				1			1			1				1
8		1			1				1												
9		1				1					1			1			1			1	
10		1				1					1			1			1			1	
11		1				1					1			1			1			1	
12		1				1					1			1			1			1	
13			1			1					1			1			1				1
14			1			1					1			1			1				1
15			1			1					1			1			1				1
16			1			1					1			1			1				1
17	0	0	0	0	0	0	0	0	0	0	0	0	0	1	1	1	1	1	1	1	1
18	1	1	1	1	0	0	0	0	0	0	0	0	0	1	1	1	0	0	0	0	0
91	0	0	0	0	0	0	0	0	0	0	0	0	0	0	0	0	0	0	0	0	0
92	0	0	0	0	0	0	0	0	0	0	0	0	0	0	0	0	0	0	0	0	0
93	0	0	0	0	0	0	0	0	0	0	0	0	0	0	0	0	0	0	0	0	0
94	1	1	1	1	1	1	1	1	1	1	1	1	1	0	0	0	0	0	0	0	0
95	0	0	0	0	0	0	0	0	0	0	0	0	0	1	1	1	1	1	1	1	1
96	0	0	0	0	1	1	1	1	1	1	1	1	1	0	0	0	1	1	1	1	1
97	1	1	1	1	0	0	0	0	0	0	0	0	0	1	1	1	0	0	0	0	0

Figure 4.18   Second half of the resultant decision table.

so, it is likely that one would overlook many of the "interesting" test cases identified by the cause–effect graph.

Since cause–effect graphing requires the translation of a specification into a Boolean logic network, it gives one a different perspective on, and additional insight into, the specification. In fact, the development of a cause–effect graph is a good way to uncover ambiguities and incompleteness in specifications. For instance, the astute reader may have noticed that this process has uncovered a problem in the specification of the DISPLAY command. The specification states that all output lines contain four words. This cannot be true in all cases; it cannot occur for test cases 18 and 26 since the starting address is less than 16 bytes away from the end of storage.

Although cause–effect graphing does produce a set of useful test cases, it normally does not produce *all* of the useful test cases that might be identified. For instance, in the example, we said nothing about verifying that the displayed storage values are identical to the values in storage, and determining if the program can display every possible value in a storage location. Also, the cause–effect graph does not adequately explore boundary conditions. Of course, one could attempt to cover boundary conditions during the process. For instance, instead of identifying the single cause

$$hexloc2 \geq hexloc1$$

one could identify two causes:

$$hexloc2 = hexloc1$$
$$hexloc2 > hexloc1$$

The problem in doing this, however, is that it complicates the graph tremendously and leads to an excessively large number of test cases. For this reason it is best to consider a separate boundary-value analysis. For instance, the following boundary conditions can be identified for the DISPLAY specification:

1. *hexloc1* has one digit
2. *hexloc1* has six digits
3. *hexloc1* has seven digits
4. $hexloc1 = 0$
5. $hexloc1 = 7FFF$
6. $hexloc1 = 8000$
7. *hexloc2* has one digit
8. *hexloc2* has six digits
9. *hexloc2* has seven digits
19. $hexloc2 = 0$
11. $hexloc2 = 7FFF$
12. $hexloc2 = 8000$
13. $hexloc2 = hexloc1$
14. $hexloc2 = hexloc1 + 1$
15. $hexloc2 = hexloc1 - 1$
16. *bytecount* has one digit
17. *bytecount* has six digits
18. *bytecount* has seven digits
19. $bytecount = 1$
20. $hexloc1 + bytecount = 8000$
21. $hexloc1 + bytecount = 8001$

22.   display 16 bytes (one line)
23.   display 17 bytes (two lines)

Note that this does not imply that one would write 60 (37 + 23) test cases. Since the cause–effect graph gives us leeway in selecting specific values for operands, the boundary conditions could be blended into the test cases derived from the cause–effect graph. In this example, by rewriting some of the original 37 test cases, all 23 boundary conditions could be covered without any additonal test cases. Thus we arrive at a small, but potent, set of test cases satisfying both objectives.

Note that cause–effect graphing is consistent with several of the testing principles in Chapter 2. Identifying the expected output of each test case is an inherent part of the technique (each column in the decision table indicates the expected effects). Also note that it encourages us to look for unwanted side effects. For instance, column (test) 1 specifies that one should expect effect 91 to be present *and* that effects 92–97 should be absent.

The most difficult aspect of the technique is the conversion of the graph into the decision table. This process is algorithmic, implying that one could automate it by writing a program. The IBM Corporation has several such programs, although they are proprietary.

For an additional example of cause–effect graphing, see reference 2.

ERROR GUESSING

It has often been noted that some people seem to be naturally adept at program testing. Without using any particular methodology such as boundary-value analysis or cause–effect graphing, these people seem to have a knack for "smelling out" errors.

One explanation of this is that these people are practicing, subconsciously more often than not, a test-case-design technique that could be termed *error guessing*. Given a particular program, they surmise, both by intuition and experience, certain probable types of errors and then write test cases to expose these errors.

It is difficult to give a procedure for the error-guessing technique since it is largely an intuitive and ad hoc process. The basic idea is to enumerate a list of possible errors or error-prone situations and then write test cases based on the list. For instance, the presence of the value 0 in a program's input or output is an error-prone situation. Therefore one might write test cases for which particular input values have a 0 value and for which particular output values are forced to 0. Also, where a variable number of inputs or outputs can be present (e.g., the number of entries in a list to be searched), the cases of "none" and "one" (e.g., empty list, list containing just one entry) are error-prone situations. Another idea is to identify test cases associated with assumptions that the programmer might have made when reading the specification (i.e., things that were omitted from the specification, either by accident or because the writer felt them to be obvious).

Since a procedure cannot be given, the next-best alternative is to discuss the spirit of error guessing, and the best way to do this is by presenting examples. If one is testing a sorting subroutine, situations to explore are:

1. The input list is empty.
2. The input list contains one entry.
3. All entries in the input list have the same value.
4. The input list is already sorted.

In other words, one enumerates those special cases that may have been overlooked when the program was designed. If one is testing a binary-search subroutine, one might try the situations where (1) there is only one entry in the table being searched, (2) the table size is a power of two (e.g., 16), and (3) the table size is one less than and one greater than a power of two (e.g., 15, 17).

Consider the MTEST program in the section on boundary-value analysis. The following additional tests come to mind when using the error-guessing technique:

1. Does the program accept "blank" as an answer?
2. A type-2 (answer) record appears in the set of type-3 (student) records.
3. A record without a 2 or 3 in the last column appears as other than the initial (title) record.
4. Two students have the same name or number.
5. Since a median is computed differently depending on whether there are an odd or even number of items, test the program for an even number of students and an odd number of students.
6. The number–of–questions field has a negative value.

Error-guessing tests that come to mind for the DISPLAY command of the previous section are

1. DISPLAY 100-   (partial second operand)
2. DISPLAY 100.   (partial second operand)
3. DISPLAY 100-10A 42   (extra operand)
4. DISPLAY 000-0000FF   (leading zeros)

THE STRATEGY

The test-case-design methodologies discussed in this chapter can be combined into an overall strategy. The reason for combining them should be obvious by now: each contributes a particular set of useful test cases, but none of them by itself contributes a thorough set of test cases. A reasonable strategy is

1. If the specification contains combinations of input conditions, start with cause–effect graphing.
2. In any event, use boundary-value analysis. Remember that this is an analysis of input *and* output boundaries. The boundary-value analysis yields a set of supplemental test conditions, but, as noted in the section on cause–effect graphing, many or all of these can be incorporated into the cause–effect tests.
3. Identify the valid and invalid equivalence classes for the input and output, and supplement the test cases identified above if necessary.
4. Use the error-guessing technique to add additional test cases.
5. Examine the program's logic with regard to the set of test cases. Use either the decision-coverage, condition-coverage, decision/condition-coverage, or multiple-condition-coverage criterion (the last being the most complete). If the coverage criterion has not been met by the test cases identified in the prior four steps, and if meeting the criterion is not impossible (i.e., certain combinations of conditions may be impossible to create because of the nature of the program), add sufficient test cases to cause the criterion to be satisfied.

Again, the use of this strategy will not guarantee that all errors will be found, but it has been found to represent a reasonable compromise. Also, it represents a considerable amount of hard work, but no one has ever claimed that program testing is easy.

REFERENCES

1. W. R. Elmendorf, "Cause-Effect Graphs in Functional Testing," TR-00.2487, IBM Systems Development Division, Poughkeepsie, N.Y., 1973.
2. G. J. Myers, *Software Reliability: Principles and Practices.* New York: Wiley–Interscience, 1976.

CHAPTER 5

Module Testing

Up to this point we have largely ignored the mechanics of testing and the size of the program being tested. However, large programs (say, programs of 500 statements or more) require special treatment in the manner in which the testing process is structured. In this chapter we consider an initial step in structuring the testing of a large program: module testing. Chapter 6 discusses the remaining steps.

Module testing (or unit testing) is a process of testing the individual subprograms, subroutines, or procedures in a program. That is, rather than initially testing the program as a whole, testing is first focused on the smaller building blocks of the program. The motivations for doing this are threefold. First, module testing is a way of managing the combinatorics of testing, since attention is focused initially on smaller units of the program. Second, module testing eases the task of debugging (the process of pinpointing and correcting a discovered error), since, when an error is found, it is known to exist in a particular module. Finally, module testing introduces parallelism into the testing process by presenting us with the opportunity to test multiple modules simultaneously.

The purpose of module testing is to compare the function of a module to some functional or interface specification defining the module. To reemphasize the goal of all testing processes, the goal here is not to show that the module meets its specification, but to show that the module contradicts the specification. The process of module testing is discussed from three points of view: the manner in which test cases are designed, the order in which modules should be tested and integrated, and some practical advice about performing the test.

TEST-CASE DESIGN

When designing test cases for a module test, two types of information must be available: a specification for the module and the module's source code. The specification typically defines the module's input and output parameters and its function.

Module testing is largely white-box oriented. One reason is that as one is testing larger entities such as entire programs (which will be the case for subsequent testing processes), white-box testing becomes less feasible. A second reason is that the subsequent testing processes are oriented toward finding different types of errors (i.e., errors not necessarily associated with the program's logic, such as the program's failing to meet its users' requirements). Hence the test-case-design procedure for a module test is the following: analyze the module's logic using one or more of the white-box methods, and then supplement these test cases by applying black-box methods to the module's specification.

Since the test-case-design methods to be used have already been defined in Chapter 4, their use in a module test is illustrated here through an example. Assume that we wish to test a module named BONUS. The function of the module is to add $200 to the salary of all employees in the department or departments having the largest sales amount. However, if an eligible employee's current salary is $15,000 or more, or if the employee is a manager, the salary should be increased by only $100.

The inputs to the module are the tables shown in Figure 5.1. If the module performs its function correctly, it returns an error code of 0. If either the employee or department table contain no entries, it returns an error code of 1. If it finds no employees in an eligible department, it returns an error code of 2.

The module's source code is shown in Figure 5.2. Input parameters ESIZE and DSIZE contain the number of entries in the employee and department tables. The module is written in PL/I,

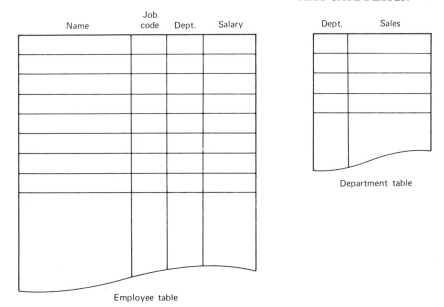

Figure 5.1   **Input tables to module BONUS.**

but the following discussion is largely language independent; the techniques are applicable to programs coded in other languages. Also, since the PL/I logic in the module is rather simple, it should be understandable by readers who are not familiar with PL/I.

Regardless of which of the logic-coverage techniques is to be used, the first step is to list the conditional decisions in the program. Candidates in this program are all IF and DO statements. By inspecting the program, we can see that all of the DO statements are simple iterations, each iteration limit will be equal to or greater than the initial value (meaning that each loop body will always execute at least once), and the only way of exiting from each loop is via the DO statement. Thus the DO statements in this program need no special attention, since any test case that causes a DO statement to execute will eventually cause it to branch in both directions (i.e., enter the loop body and skip the loop body). Therefore, the statements that must be analyzed are

```
2 IF (ESIZE<=0)l(DSIZE<=0)
6 IF (SALES (I)>=MAXSALES)
9 IF (SALES (J)=MAXSALES)
13 IF (EMPTAB.DEPT (K)=DEPTTAB.DEPT (J))
16 IF (SALARY (K) > = LSALARY)l(CODE (K) = MGR)
21 IF (¬ FOUND)
```

```
BONUS: PROCEDURE (EMPTAB,DEPTTAB,ESIZE,DSIZE,ERRCODE) ;
DECLARE 1 EMPTAB (*),
          2 NAME CHAR (6),
          2 CODE CHAR (1),
          2 DEPT CHAR (3),
          2 SALARY FIXED DECIMAL(7,2);
DECLARE 1 DEPTTAB (*),
          2 DEPT CHAR (3),
          2 SALES FIXED DECIMAL(8,2);
DECLARE (ESIZE,DSIZE) FIXED BINARY;
DECLARE ERRCODE FIXED DECIMAL(1);
DECLARE MAXSALES FIXED DECIMAL(8,2) INIT(0); /*MAX. SALES IN DEPTTAB*/
DECLARE (I,J,K) FIXED BINARY;                /*COUNTERS*/
DECLARE FOUND BIT(1);     /*TRUE IF ELIGIBLE DEPT. HAS EMPLOYEES*/
DECLARE SINC FIXED DECIMAL(7,2) INIT(200.00); /*STANDARD INCREMENT*/
DECLARE LINC FIXED DECIMAL(7,2) INIT(100.00); /*LOWER INCREMENT*/
DECLARE LSALARY FIXED DECIMAL(7,2) INIT(15000.00); /*SALARY BOUNDARY*/
DECLARE MGR CHAR(1) INIT('M');

 1   ERRCODE=0;
 2   IF(ESIZE<=0) | (DSIZE<=0)
 3    THEN ERRCODE=1;                    /*EMPTAB OR DEPTTAB ARE EMPTY*/
 4    ELSE DO;
 5            DO I = 1 TO DSIZE;         /*FIND MAXSALES AND MAXDEPTS*/
 6              IF(SALES(I)>=MAXSALES) THEN MAXSALES=SALES(I);
 7            END;
 8            DO J = 1 TO DSIZE;
 9              IF(SALES(J)=MAXSALES)     /*ELIGIBLE DEPARTMENT*/
10                THEN DO;
11                        FOUND='0'B;
12                        DO K = 1 TO ESIZE;
13                          IF(EMPTAB.DEPT(K)=DEPTTAB.DEPT(J))
14                            THEN DO;
15                                    FOUND='1'B;
16                                    IF(SALARY(K)>=LSALARY) | (CODE(K)=MGR)
17                                      THEN SALARY(K)=SALARY(K)+LINC;
18                                      ELSE SALARY(K)=SALARY(K)+SINC;
19                                 END;
20                        END;
21                        IF(¬FOUND) THEN ERRCODE=2;
22                    END;
23            END;
24        END;
25   END;
```

Figure 5.2   **Module BONUS.**

Given the small number of decisions, we should probably opt for multicondition coverage, but we shall examine all the logic-coverage criteria (except statement coverage, which is always too limited to be of use) to see their effects.

To satisfy the decision-coverage criterion, we need sufficient test cases to evoke both outcomes of each of the six decisions. The required input situations to evoke all decision outcomes are listed in Table 5.1. Since two of the outcomes will always occur, there are 10 situations that need to be forced by test cases. Note that, to construct Table 5.1, decision-outcome circumstances had to be traced back through the logic of the program to determine the proper corresponding input circumstances. For instance, decision 16 is not evoked by *any* employee meeting the conditions; the employee must be in an eligible department.

Table 5.1   Situations Corresponding to the Decision Outcomes

Decision	True outcome	False outcome
2	ESIZE or DSIZE ≤ 0	ESIZE and DSIZE > 0
6	Will always occur at least once	Order DEPTTAB so that a department with lower sales occurs after a department with higher sales.
9	Will always occur at least once	All departments do not have the same sales
13	There is an employee in an eligible department	There is an employee who is not in an eligible department
16	An eligible employee is either a manager or earns LSALARY or more	An eligible employee is not a manager and earns less than LSALARY
21	All eligible department contains no employees	An eligible department contains at least one employee

The 10 situations of interest in Table 5.1 could be evoked by the 2 test cases in Figure 5.3. Note that each test case includes a definition of the expected output, in adherence with the principles discussed in Chapter 2.

Although these two test cases meet the decision-coverage criterion, it should be obvious that there could be many types of errors in the module that are not detected by these two test

Test case	Input	Expected output
1	ESIZE = 0 All other inputs are irrelevant.	ERRCODE = 1 ESIZE, DSIZE, EMPTAB, and DEPTTAB are unchanged.
2	ESIZE = DSIZE = 3 EMPTAB JONES E D42 21,000.00 SMITH E D32 14,000.00 LORIN E D42 10,000.00 DEPTTAB D42 10,000.00 D32 8,000.00 D95 10,000.00	ERRCODE = 2 ESIZE, DSIZE, and DEPTTAB are unchanged. EMPTAB JONES E D42 21,100.00 SMITH E D32 14,000.00 LORIN E D42 10,200.00

Figure 5.3   **Test cases to satisfy the decision–coverage criterion.**

Table 5.2   Situations Corresponding to Condition Outcomes

Decision	Condition	True outcome	False outcome
2	ESIZE $\leq$ 0	ESIZE $\leq$ 0	ESIZE $>$ 0
2	DSIZE $\leq$ 0	DSIZE $\leq$ 0	DSIZE $>$0
6	SALES (I) $\geq$ MAXSALES	Will always occur at least once	Order DEPTTAB so that a department with lower sales occurs after a department with higher sales
9	SALES (J) = MAXSALES	Will always occur at least once	All departments do not have the same sales
13	EMPTAB.DEPT (K) = DEPTTAB. DEPT (J)	There is an employee in an eligible department	There is an employee who is not in an eligible department
16	SALARY (K) $\geq$ LSALARY	An eligible employee earns LSALARY or more.	An eligible employee earns less than LSALARY.
16	CODE (K) = MGR	An eligible employee is a manager	An eligible employee is not a manager
21	$\neg$ FOUND	An eligible department contains no employees	An eligible department contains at least one employee

cases. For instance, the test cases do not explore the circumstances where the error code is 0, an employee is a manager, or the department table is empty (DSIZE$\leq$0).

A more satisfactory test can be obtained by the use of the condition-coverage criterion. Here we need sufficient test cases to evoke both outcomes of each condition in the decisions. The conditions and the required input situations to evoke all outcomes are listed in Table 5.2. Since two of the outcomes will always occur, there are 14 situations that must be forced by test cases. Again, these situations can be evoked by only two test cases, as shown in Figure 5.4.

The test cases in Figure 5.4 were designed to illustrate a problem. Since they do evoke all the outcomes in Table 5.2, they satisfy the condition-coverage criterion, but they are probably a

Test case	Input	Expected output
1	ESIZE = DSIZE = 0 All other inputs are irrelevant.	ERRCODE = 1 ESIZE, DSIZE, EMPTAB, and DEPTTAB are unchanged
2	ESIZE = DSIZE = 3 EMPTAB JONES E D42 21,000.00 SMITH E D32 14,000.00 LORIN M D42 10,000.00 DEPTTAB D42 10,000.00 D32 8,000.00 D95 10,000.00	ERRCODE = 2 ESIZE, DSIZE, and DEPTTAB are unchanged. EMPTAB JONES E D42 21,100.00 SMITH E D32 14,000.00 LORIN M D42 10,100.00

Figure 5.4   **Test cases to satisfy the condition–coverage criterion.**

poorer set of test cases than those in Figure 5.3 satisfying the decision-coverage criterion. The reason is that they do not cause every statement to be executed; statement 18 is never executed. Moreover, they do not accomplish much more than the test cases in Figure 5.3. They do not cause the output situation ERRCODE=0. If statement 2 had erroneously said (ESIZE=0) & (DSIZE=0), this error would go undetected. Of course, an alternative set of test cases might solve these problems, but the fact remains that the two test cases in Figure 5.4 do satisfy the condition-coverage criterion.

The big weakness in the test cases in Figure 5.4 would be eliminated by using the decision/condition-coverage criterion. Here we would provide sufficient test cases such that all outcomes of all conditions *and* decisions were evoked at least once. This could be accomplished by making Jones a manager and making Lorin a nonmanager. This would have the result of generating both outcomes of decision 16, thus causing us to execute statement 18.

One problem with this, however, is that it is esentially no better than the test cases in Figure 5.3. If the compiler being used stops evaluating an *or* expression as soon as it determines that one operand is true, this modification would result in the expression CODE(K)=MGR in statement 16 never having a *true* outcome. Hence, if this expression were coded incorrectly, the test cases would not detect the error.

The last criterion to explore is multicondition coverage. This criterion requires sufficient test cases such that all possible combinations of conditions in each decision are evoked at least once. This can be accomplished by working from Table 5.2. Decisions 6,

9, 13, and 21 have two combinations each; decisions 2 and 16 have four combinations each. The methodology to design the test cases is to select one that covers as many of the combinations as possible, select another that covers as many of the remaining combinations as possible, and so on. A set of test cases satisfying the multicondition-coverage criterion is shown in Figure 5.5. The set is more comprehensive than the previous sets of test cases, implying that we should have selected this criterion at the beginning.

It is important to realize that module BONUS could have a large number of errors that would not be detected by even the tests satisfying the multicondition-coverage criterion. For instance, no test cases generate the situation where ERRCODE is returned with a value of 0; thus, if statement 1 were missing, the error would go undetected. If LSALARY was erroneously initialized to \$15,000.01, the mistake would go unnoticed. If statement 16 stated SALARY (K) > LSALARY instead of SALARY (K) > = LSALARY, this error would not be found. Also, whether a variety of off-by-one errors (e.g., not handling the last entry in DEPTTAB or EMPTAB correctly) would be detected would depend largely on chance.

Test case	Input	Expected output
1	ESIZE = 0 DSIZE = 0 All other inputs are irrelevant.	ERRCODE = 1 ESIZE, DSIZE, EMPTAB, and DEPTTAB are unchanged.
2	ESIZE = 0 DSIZE > 0 All other inputs are irrelevant.	Same as above.
3	ESIZE > 0 DSIZE = 0 All other inputs are irrelevant.	Same as above.
4	ESIZE = 5 DSIZE = 4 EMPTAB JONES M D42 21,000.00 WARNS M D95 12,000.00 LORIN E D42 10,000.00 TOY E D95 16,000.00 SMITH E D32 14,000.00 DEPTTAB D42 10,000.00 D32 8,000.00 D95 10,000.00 D44 10,000.00	ERRCODE = 2 ESIZE, DSIZE, and DEPTTAB are unchanged. EMPTAB JONES M D42 21,100.00 WARNS M D95 12,100.00 LORIN E D42 10,200.00 TOY E D95 16,100.00 SMITH E D32 14,000.00

Figure 5.5   **Test cases to satisfy the multicondition–coverage criterion.**

Two points should be apparent now: the multicondition-coverage criterion is superior to the other criteria, and *any* logic-coverage criterion is not good enough to serve as the only means of deriving module tests. Hence, the next step is to supplement the tests in Figure 5.5 with a set of black-box tests. To do so, the interface specification of BONUS is included below.

BONUS, a PL/I module, receives five parameters, symbolically referred to here as EMPTAB, DEPTTAB, ESIZE, DSIZE, and ERRCODE. The attributes of these parameters are

```
DECLARE 1 EMPTAB (*),                    /*INPUT AND OUTPUT*/
          2 NAME CHARACTER (6),
          2 CODE CHARACTER (1),
          2 DEPT CHARACTER (3),
          2 SALARY FIXED DECIMAL (7,2);
DECLARE 1 DEPTTAB (*),                   /*INPUT*/
          2 DEPT CHARACTER (3),
          2 SALES FIXED DECIMAL (8,2);
DECLARE (ESIZE,DSIZE) FIXED BINARY;      /*INPUT*/
DECLARE ERRCODE FIXED DECIMAL (1);       /*OUTPUT*/
```

The module assumes that the transmitted arguments have these attributes. ESIZE and DSIZE indicate the number of entries in EMPTAB and DEPTTAB, respectively. No assumptions should be made about the order of entries in EMPTAB and DETTAB. The function of the module is to increment the salary (EMPTAB.SALARY) of those employees in the department or departments having the largest sales amount (DEPTTAB.SALES). If an eligible employee's current salary is $15,000.00 or more, or if the employee is a manager (EMPTAB.CODE='M'), the increment is $100; if not, the increment for the eligible employee is $200. The module assumes that the incremented salary will fit into field EMPTAB.SALARY. If ESIZE and DSIZE are not greater than 0, ERRCODE is set to 1 and no further action is taken. In all other cases, the function is completely performed. However, if a maximum-sales department is found to have no employee, processing continues, but ERRCODE will have the value 2; otherwise it is set to 0.

This specification is not suited to cause–effect graphing (there is not a discernable set of input conditions whose combinations should be explored); thus boundary-value analysis will be used. The input boundaries identified are

1. EMPTAB has 1 entry.
2. EMPTAB has the maximum number of entries (65535).
3. EMPTAB has 0 entries.
4. DEPTTAB has 1 entry.
5. DEPTTAB has 65535 entries.
6. DEPTTAB has 0 entries.
7. A maximum-sales department has 1 employee.
8. A maximum-sales department has 65535 employees.
9. A maximum-sales department has no employees.
10. All departments in DEPTTAB have the same sales.
11. The maximum-sales department is the first entry in DEPTTAB.
12. The maximum-sales department is the last entry in DEPTTAB.
13. An eligible employee is the first entry in EMPTAB.
14. An eligible employee is the last entry in EMPTAB.
15. An eligible employee is a manager.
16. An eligible employee is not a manager.
17. An eligible employee who is not a manager has a salary of $14,999.99.
18. An eligible employee who is not a manager has a salary of $15,000.00.
19. An eligible employee who is not a manager has a salary of $15,000.01.

The output boundaries are

20. ERRCODE = 0.
21. ERRCODE = 1.
22. ERRCODE = 2.
23. The incremented salary of an eligible employee is $99,999.99 (maximum).

A further test condition based on the error-guessing technique is

24. A maximum-sales department with no employees is followed in DEPTTAB with another maximum-sales department having employees.

This is used to determine whether the module erroneously terminates processing of the input when it encounters an ERRCODE=2 situation.

Reviewing these 24 conditions, conditions 2, 5, and 8 seem like impractical test cases. Since they also represent conditions that will never occur (usually a dangerous assumption to make when testing, but seemingly safe here), they are excluded. The next step is to compare the remaining 21 conditions to the current set of test cases (Figure 5.5) to determine which boundary conditions are not already covered. Doing so, we see that conditions 1, 4, 7, 10, 14, 17, 18, 19, 20, 23, and 24 require test cases beyond those in Figure 5.5.

The next step is to design additional test cases to cover these 11 boundary conditions. One approach is to merge these conditions into the existing test cases (i.e., by modifying test case 4 in Figure 5.5), but this is not recommended because doing so could inadvertently upset the complete multicondition coverage of the existing test cases. Hence the safest approach is to add test cases to those of Figure 5.5. In doing this, the goal is to design the smallest number of test cases necessary to cover the boundary conditions. The three test cases in Figure 5.6 accomplish this. Test case 5 covers conditions 7, 10, 14, 17, 18, 19, and 20; test case 6 covers conditions 1, 4, and 23; and test case 7 covers condition 24.

The premise here is that the logic-coverage, or white-box, test cases in Figure 5.5 and the black-box test cases in Figure 5.6 form a reasonable module test for procedure BONUS.

INCREMENTAL TESTING

In performing the process of module testing, there are two key considerations: the design of an effective set of test cases, which was discussed in the previous section, and the manner in which the modules are combined to form a working program. The second consideration is important because it has implications on the form in which module test cases are written, the types of test tools that might be used, the order in which modules are coded and tested, the cost of generating test cases, and the cost of debugging (locating and repairing detected errors). In short, then, it is a consideration of considerable importance. In this section, two approaches, incremental and nonincremental testing, are discussed. In the next section, two incremental approaches, top-down and bottom-up development or testing, are explored.

Test case	Input	Expected output
5	ESIZE = 3 DSIZE = 2 EMPTAB ALLY | E | D36 | 14,999.99 BEST | E | D33 | 15,000.00 CELTO | E | D33 | 15,000.01 DEPTTAB D33 | 55,400.01 D36 | 55,400.01	ERRCODE = 0 ESIZE, DSIZE, and DEPTTAB are unchanged. EMPTAB ALLY | E | D36 | 15,199.99 BEST | E | D33 | 15,100.00 CELTO | E | D33 | 15,100.01
6	ESIZE = 1 DSIZE = 1 EMPTAB CHIEF | M | D99 | 99,899.99 DEPTTAB D99 | 99,000.00	ERRCODE = 0 ESIZE, DSIZE, and DEPTTAB are unchanged. EMPTAB CHIEF | M | D99 | 99,999.99
7	ESIZE = 2 DSIZE = 2 EMPTAB DOLE | E | D67 | 10,000.00 FORD | E | D22 | 33,333.33 DEPTTAB D66 | 20,000.00 D67 | 20,000.00	ERRCODE = 2 ESIZE, DSIZE, and DEPTTAB are unchanged. EMPTAB DOLE | E | D67 | 10,200.00 FORD | E | D22 | 33,333.33

Figure 5.6 **Supplemental boundary–value–analysis test cases for BONUS.**

The question explored here is the following: Should one test a program by testing each module independently and then combining the modules to form the program, or should one combine the next module to be tested with the set of previously tested modules before it is tested? The first approach is called *nonincremental* or "big-bang" testing or integration; the second approach is known as *incremental* testing or integration.

The program in Figure 5.7 is used as an example. The rectangles represent the six modules (subroutines or procedures) in the program. The lines connecting the modules represent the control hierarchy of the program; that is, module A calls modules B, C, and D; module B calls module E; and so on. Nonincremental testing, the traditional approach, is performed in the following manner. First, a module test is performed on each of the six modules, testing each module as a stand-alone entity. The modules might be tested at the same time or tested in succession, depending on the environment (e.g., interactive versus batch-processing computing facilities) and the number of people involved. Finally, the modules are combined or integrated (e.g., "link edited") to form the program.

The testing of each module requires a special *driver module* and one or more *stub modules.* For instance, to test module B, test cases are first designed and then fed to module B by passing it input arguments from a driver module, a small module that must be coded to "drive" or transmit test cases through the module under test. (Alternatively, a test tool could be used.) The driver module must also display, to the tester, the results produced by B. In addition, since module B calls module E, something must be present to receive control when B calls E. This is accomplished by a stub module, a special module given the name "E" that must be coded to simulate the function of module E. When the module testing of all six modules has been completed, the modules are combined to form the program.

The alternative approach is incremental testing. Rather than testing each module in isolation, the next module to be tested is first combined with the set of modules that have already been tested.

It is premature to give a procedure for incrementally testing the program in Figure 5.7, because there are a large number of possible incremental approaches. A key issue is whether we should begin at the top or bottom of the program. However, since this issue is discussed in the next section, let us assume for the

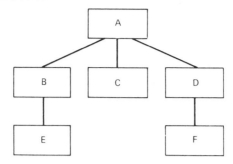

Figure 5.7   Sample 6–module program.

moment that we are beginning from the bottom. The first step is to test modules E, C, and F, either in parallel (e.g., by three people) or serially. Notice that we must prepare a driver for each module, but not a stub. The next step is the testing of B and D, but rather than testing them in isolation, they are combined with modules E and F, respectively. In other words, to test module B, a driver is written, incorporating the test cases, and the pair B–E is tested. The incremental process, adding the next module to the set or subset of previously tested modules, is continued until the last module (module A in this case) is tested. Note that this procedure could have alternatively progressed from the top to the bottom.

Several observations should be apparent at this point:

1. Nonincremental testing requires more work. For the program in Figure 5.7, five drivers and five stubs must be prepared (assuming we do not need a driver module for the top module). The bottom-up incremental test would require five drivers but no stubs. A top-down incremental test would require five stubs but no drivers. Less work is required because previously tested modules are used instead of the driver modules (if one starts from the top) or stub modules (if one starts from the bottom) needed in the nonincremental approach.

2. Programming errors related to mismatching interfaces or incorrect assumptions among modules will be detected earlier if incremental testing is used. The reason is that combinations of modules are tested together at an early point in time. However, if nonimcremental testing is used, modules do not "see one another" until the end of the process.

3. As a result, debugging should be easier if incremental testing

is used. If we assume that errors related to intermodule interfaces and assumptions do exist (a good assumption from experience), then, if nonincremental testing has been used, the errors will not surface until the entire program has been combined. At this time, we may have difficulty pinpointing the error, since it could be anywhere within the program. Conversely, if incremental testing is used, an error of this type should be easier to pinpoint, because it is likely that the error is associated with the most recently added module.

4. Incremental testing might result in more thorough testing. If one is testing module B, either module E or A (depending on whether one started from the bottom or the top) is executed as a result. Although E or A should have been thoroughly tested previously, perhaps executing it as a result of B's module test will evoke a new condition, perhaps one that represents a deficiency in the original test of E or A. On the other hand, if nonincremental testing is used, the testing of B will affect only module B. In other words, incremental testing substitutes previously tested modules for the stubs or drivers needed in the nonincremental test. As a result, the actual modules receive more "exposure" by the completion of the last module test.

5. As a result, the nonincremental approach appears to use less machine time. If module A of Figure 5.7 is being tested using the bottom-up incremental approach, modules B, C, D, E, and F probably execute during the execution of A. In a nonincremental test of A, only stubs for B, C, and D are executed. The same is true for a top-down incremental test. If module F is being tested, modules A, B, C, D, and E may be executed during the test of F; in the nonincremental test of F, only the driver for F, plus F itself, executes. Hence, the number of machine instructions executed during a test run using the incremental approach is apparently greater than that for the nonincremental approach. However, offsetting this is the fact that the nonincremental test requires more drivers and stubs than the incremental test; machine time is needed to develop the drivers and stubs.

6. At the beginning of the module-testing phase, there is more opportunity for parallel activities if nonincremental testing is used (i.e., all the modules can be tested simultaneously). This might be of significance in a large project (many modules and people), since the headcount of a project is usually at its peak at the start of the module-test phase.

In summary, observations 1–4 are advantages of incremental testing, and observations 5–6 are disadvantages. Given current trends in the computing industry (hardware costs are decreasing, and labor costs and the consequences of software errors are increasing), and given the fact that the earlier an error is found, the lower the cost of repairing it, one sees that observations 1–4 are increasing in importance while observation 5 is becoming less important. Observation 6 seems to be a weak disadvantage, if one at all. This leads to the conclusion that incremental testing is superior.

TOP-DOWN VERSUS BOTTOM-UP TESTING

Given the conclusion of the previous section, that incremental testing is superior to nonincremental testing, two incremental strategies are explored: *top-down* and *bottom-up* testing. Before discussing them, however, several misconceptions should be clarified. First, the terms "top-down testing," "top-down development," and "top-down design" are often used as synonyms. Top-down testing and top-down development are synonyms (they represent a strategy of ordering the coding and testing of modules), but top-down design is something quite different and independent. A program that was designed in a top-down fashion can be incrementally tested in either a top-down or a bottom-up fashion.

Second, bottom-up testing (or bottom-up development) is often mistakenly equated with nonincremental testing. The reason is that bottom-up testing begins in a manner that is identical to a nonincremental test (i.e., when the bottom, or terminal, modules are tested), but as we saw in the previous section, bottom-up testing is an incremental strategy. Finally, since both strategies are incremental, the advantages of incremental testing are not repeated here; only the differences between top-down and bottom-up testing are discussed.

Top-Down Testing

The top-down strategy starts with the top, or initial, module in the program. After this, there is no single "right" procedure for selecting the next module to be incrementally tested; the only rule is that to be eligible to be the next module, at least one of the module's superordinate (calling) modules must have been tested previously.

Figure 5.8 is used to illustrate the strategy. A–L are the 12 modules in the program. Assume that module J contains the program's I/O read operations and module I contains the write operations.

The first step is the testing of module A. To accomplish this, stub modules representing B, C, and D must be written. Unfortunately, the production of stub modules is often misunderstood; as evidence, one often sees such statements as "a stub module need only write a message stating 'we got this far,'" and "in many cases, the dummy module [stub] simply exits—without doing any work at all." In most situations, these statements are false. Since module A calls module B, A is expecting B to perform some work; this work most likely is some result (e.g., output arguments) returned to A. If the stub simply returns control or writes an error message without returning a meaningful result, module A will fail, not because of an error in A, but because of a failure of the stub to simulate the corresponding module. Moreover, returning a "wired-in" output from a stub module is often insufficient. For instance, consider the task of writing a stub representing a square-root routine, a table-search routine, an "obtain corresponding master-file record" routine, and the like. If the stub returns a fixed wired-in output, but not having the particular value expected by the calling module during this invocation, the

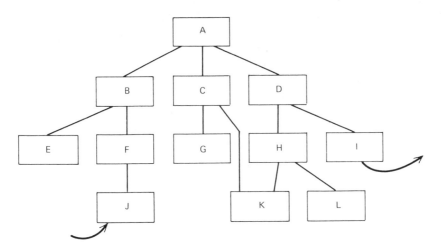

Figure 5.8   Sample 12–module program.

calling module may fail or produce a confusing result. Hence the production of stubs is not a trivial task.

Another consideration is the form in which test cases are presented to the program, an important consideration that is not even mentioned in most discussion of top-down testing. In our example, the question is: how does one feed test cases to module A? Since the top module in typical programs neither receives input arguments or performs input/output operations, the answer is not immediately obvious. The answer is that the test data are fed to the module (module A in this situation) from one or more of its stubs. To illustrate, assume that the functions of B, C, and D are

B—Obtain summary of transaction file.

C—Determine whether weekly status meets quota.

D—Produce weekly summary report.

A test case for A, then, is a transaction summary returned from stub B. Stub D might contain statements to write its input data to a printer or terminal, allowing the results of each test to be examined.

In this program, another problem exists. Since module A presumably calls B only once, the problem is how one feeds more than one test case to A. One solution is to develop multiple versions of stub B, each with a different "wired-in" set of test data to be returned to A. To execute the test cases, the program is executed multiple times, each time with a different version of stub B. Another alternative is to place test data on external files and have stub B read the test data and return them to A. In either case, and because of the previous discussion, one sees that the development of stub modules is more difficult than it is often made out to be. Furthermore, it is often necessary, because of the characteristics of the program, to represent a test case across multiple stubs beneath the module under test (i.e., where the module receives data to be acted upon by calling multiple modules).

After A has been tested, one of the stubs is replaced by an actual module, and the stubs required by that module are added. For instance, Figure 5.9 might represent the next version of the program.

After testing the top module, numerous sequences are possible. For instance, if we are performing all the testing sequentially, a few of the many possible sequences of modules are

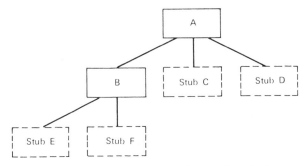

Figure 5.9   **Second step in the top–down test.**

A   B   C   D   E   F   G   H   I   J   K   L

A   B   E   F   J   C   G   K   D   H   L   I

A   D   H   I   K   L   C   G   B   F   J   E

A   B   F   J   D   I   E   C   G   K   H   L

If parallel testing occurs, other alternatives are possible. For instance, after module A has been tested, one programmer could take module A and test the combination A–B, another programmer could test A–C, and a third could test A–D. In general, there is no best sequence, but two guidelines to consider are.

1. If there are critical sections of the program (perhaps module G), design the sequence such that these sections are added as early as possible. A "critical section" might be a complex module, a module with a new algorithm, or a module suspected to be error prone.
2. Design the sequence such that the I/O modules are added as early as possible.

The motivation for the first should be obvious, but the motivation for the second deserves further discussion. Recall that a problem with stubs was that some of them must contain the test cases and others must write their input to a printer or terminal. However, as soon as the module accepting the program's input is added, the representation of test cases is considerably simplified; their form is identical to the input accepted by the final program (e.g., from a transaction file or a terminal). Likewise, once the module performing the program's output function is added, the placement of code in stub modules to write results of test cases might no longer be necessary. Thus, if modules J and I are the I/O modules and if module G performs some critical function, the incremental sequence might be

A   B   F   J   D   I   C   G   E   K   H   L

and the form of the program after the sixth increment would be that in Figure 5.10.

Once the intermediate state in Figure 5.10 has been reached, the representation of test cases and the inspection of results is simplified. It has other advantages as well. At this point one has a working skeletal version of the program, that is, a version that performs actual input and output operations, although some of its "insides" are still being simulated by stubs. This early skeletal version allows one to find human-factor errors and problems, allows the program to be demonstrated to the eventual user, serves as evidence that the overall design of the program is sound, and, to some, serves as a morale booster. These points represent the major advantages of the top-down strategy.

On the other hand, the top-down approach has some serious shortcomings. Assume that our current state of testing is that of Figure 5.10 and that our next step is to replace stub H with module H. What we should do at this point (or earlier) is use the methods described earlier in this chapter to design a set of test cases for H. Note, however, that the test cases are in the form of

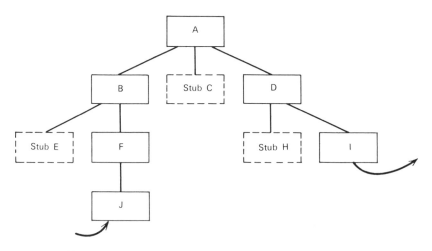

Figure 5.10   **Intermediate state in the top–down test.**

actual program inputs to module J. This presents two problems. First, because of the intervening modules between J and H (F, B, A, and D), we might find it *impossible* to represent certain test cases to module J that test every predefined situation in H. For instance, if H is the BONUS module of Figure 5.2, it might be impossible, because of the nature of intervening module D, to create some of the seven test cases of Figures 5.5 and 5.6. Second, because of the "distance" between H and the point at which the test data enter the program, even if it is possible to test every situation, determining what data to feed to J to test these situations in H is often a difficult mental task.

A third problem is that, because the displayed output of a test might come from a module that is a large distance away from the module being tested, correlating the displayed output to what went on in the module may be difficult, occasionally even impossible. Consider adding module E to Figure 5.10. The results of each test case are determined by examining the output written by module I, but because of the intervening modules, it may be difficult to deduce the actual output of E (i.e., the data returned to B).

The top-down strategy, depending on how it is approached, may have two further problems. People occasionally feel that it can be overlapped with the program's design. For instance, if one is in the process of designing the program in Figure 5.8, one might believe that after the first two levels are designed, modules A–D can be coded and tested while the design of the lower levels progresses. As this author has emphasized elsewhere [1], this is usually an unwise decision. Program design is an iterative process, meaning that when we are designing the lower levels of a program's structure, we may discover desirable changes or improvements to the upper levels. If the upper levels have already been coded and tested, the desirable improvements will most likely be discarded, an unwise decision in the long run.

A final problem that often arises in practice is not completely testing a module before proceeding to another module. This arises for two reasons: because of the difficulty of imbedding test data in stub modules, and because the upper levels of a program usually provide resources to lower levels. In Figure 5.8 we saw that testing module A might require multiple versions of the stub for module B. In practice, there is a tendency to say, "Because this represents a lot of work, I won't execute all of A's test cases now. I'll wait until I place module J in the program, at which time the representation of test cases is easier, and remember at this point to finish testing module A." Of course, the problem here is that we may forget to test the remainder of module A at this later point in time. Also, because upper levels often provide resources for use by lower levels (e.g., opening of files), it is difficult sometimes to determine if the resources have been provided correctly (e.g., if a file has been opened with the proper attributes) until the lower modules that use them are tested.

Bottom-Up Testing

The next step is to examine the bottom-up incremental testing strategy. For the most part, bottom-up testing is the opposite of top-down testing; the advantages of top-down testing become the disadvantages of bottom-up testing, and the disadvantages of top-down testing become the advantages of bottom-up testing. Because of this, the discussion of bottom-up testing is shorter.

The bottom-up strategy starts with the terminal modules in the program (the modules that do not call other modules). After these modules have been tested, again there is no "best" procedure for selecting the next module to be incrementally tested; the only rule is that, to be eligible to be the next module, all of the module's subordinate modules (the modules it calls) must have been tested previously.

Returning to Figure 5.8, the first step is to test some or all of modules E, J, G, K, L, and I, either serially or in parallel. To do so, each module needs a special driver module: a module that contains wired-in test inputs, calls the module being tested, and displays the outputs (or compares the actual outputs with the expected outputs). Unlike the situation with stubs, multiple versions of a driver are not needed, since the driver module can iteratively call the module being tested. In most cases, driver modules are easier to produce than stub modules.

As was the case earlier, a factor influencing the sequence of testing is the critical nature of the modules. If we decide that modules D and F are most critical, an intermediate state of the bottom-up incremental test might be that of Figure 5.11. The next steps might be to test E and then test B, combining B with the previously tested modules E, F, and J.

A drawback of the bottom-up strategy is that there is no concept of an early skeletal program. In fact, the working program does not exist until the last module (module A) is added, and this working program is the complete program. Although the I/O functions can be tested before the whole program has been integrated (the I/O modules are being used in Figure 5.11), the advantages of the early skeletal program are not present.

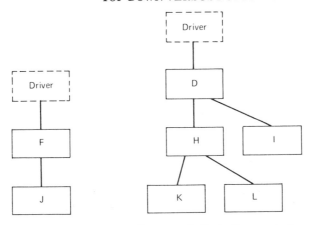

Figure 5.11   **Intermediate state in the bottom–up test.**

The problems associated with the impossibility or difficulty of creating all test situations in the top-down approach do not exist here. If one thinks of a driver module as a test probe, the probe is being placed directly on the module being tested; there are no intervening modules to worry about. Examining other problems associated with the top-down approach, one cannot make the unwise decision to overlap design and testing, since the bottom-up test cannot begin until the bottom of the program has been designed. Also, the problem of not completing the test of a module before starting another, because of the difficulty of encoding test data in multiple versions of a stub, does not exist when using bottom-up testing.

A Comparison

It would be convenient if the top-down versus bottom-up issue were as clearcut as the incremental versus nonincremental issue, but unfortunately it is not. Table 5.3 summarizes their relative advantages and disadvantages (excluding the previously discussed advantages shared by both—the advantages of incremental testing). The first advantage of each approach might appear to be the deciding factor, but there is no evidence showing that major flaws occur more often at the top or bottom levels of the typical program. The safest way to make a decision is to weigh the factors in Table 5.3 with respect to the particular program being tested. Lacking such a program here, the serious consequences of the fourth disadvantage of top-down testing,

Table 5.3   Comparison of Top-Down and Bottom-Up Testing

Top-Down Testing	
Advantages	Disadvantages
1. Advantageous if major flaws occur toward the top of the program 2. Once the I/O functions are added, representation of test cases is easier 3. Early skeletal program allows demonstrations and boosts morale	1. Stub modules must be produced 2. Stub modules are often more complicated than they first appear to be 3. Before the I/O functions are added, the representation of test cases in stubs can be difficult 4. Test conditions may be impossible, or very difficult, to create 5. Observation of test output is more difficult 6. Allows one to think that design and testing can be overlapped 7. Induces one to defer completion of the testing of certain modules
Bottom-Up Testing	
1. Advantageous if major flaws occur toward the bottom of the program 2. Test conditions are easier to create 3. Observation of test results is easier	1. Driver modules must be produced 2. The program as an entity does not exist until the last module is added

and the availability of test tools that eliminate the need for drivers, but not stubs, seem to give the bottom-up strategy the edge.

In addition, it may be apparent that top-down and bottom-up testing are not the only possible incremental strategies. Reference 2 describes three other alternative strategies.

PERFORMING THE TEST

The remaining part of the module test is the act of actually carrying out the test. A set of hints and guidelines for doing this are described below.

When a test case produces a situation where the module's actual results do not match the expected results, there are two possible explanations: either the module contains an error, or the expected results are incorrect (the test case is incorrect). To minimize this confusion, the set of test cases should be reviewed or inspected before the test is performed (i.e., the test cases should be "tested").

The use of automated test tools can minimize part of the drudgery of the testing process; such tools are surveyed in Chapter 8. For instance, there exist test tools that eliminate the need for driver modules. Flow-analysis tools enumerate the paths through a program, find statements that can never be executed ("unreachable" code), and find instances where a variable is used before it is assigned a value.

It is helpful, when preparing for a module test, to review the psychological and economic principles discussed in Chapter 2. As was the practice earlier in this chapter, remember that a definition of the expected result is a necessary part of a test case. When executing a test, remember to look for side effects (instances where a module does something it is not supposed to do). In general these situations are difficult to detect, but some instances may be found by checking, after execution of the test case, the inputs to the module that are not supposed to be altered. For instance, test case 7 in Figure 5.6 states that, as part of the expected result, ESIZE, DSIZE, and DEPTTAB should be unchanged. When running this test case, not only is the output examined for the correct result, but ESIZE, DSIZE, and DEPT-TAB should be examined to determine if they were erroneously altered.

The psychological problems associated with a person attempting to test his or her own programs apply to module testing. Rather than testing their own modules, programmers might swap modules; the programmer of the calling module is always a good candidate to test a module. Note that this applies only to *testing*; the *debugging* of a module should always be performed by the original programmer. Avoid throw-away test cases; represent them in such a form that they can be reused in the future. Recall the counterintuitive phenomenon in Figure 2.2. If an abnormally high number of errors is found in a subset of the modules, it is likely that these modules contain even more, as yet undetected, errors. Such modules should be subjected to further module testing, and possibly an additional code walkthrough or inspection. Finally, remember that the purpose of a module test is not to demonstrate that the module functions correctly, but to demonstrate the presence of errors in the module.

REFERENCES

1. G. J. Myers, *Composite/Structured Design*. New York: Van Nostrand Reinhold, 1978.
2. G. J. Myers, *Software Reliability: Principles and Practices*. New York: Wiley–Interscience, 1976.

CHAPTER 6

Higher-Order Testing

After the module testing of a program has been completed, the testing process is really only just beginning, particularly if the program is large or if it represents a product. One reason is the following definition of a software error [1]:

A software error is present when the program does not do what its end user reasonably expects it to do.

Obviously, even if an absolutely perfect module test could be performed, it in no way would guarantee that all software errors, using this definition, will be found. Hence we see one reason why some form of further testing is necessary.

A further reason for the necessity of "higher-order" types of testing is based on a premise describing how software errors originate. The premise [1] is that software development is largely a process of communicating information about the eventual program and translating this information from one form to another, and that the vast majority of software errors are attributable to breakdowns, mistakes, and noise during the communication and translation of information.

This view of software development is illustrated in Figure 6.1, a model of the development cycle for a software product. The flow of the process can be summarized in seven steps:

1. The needs of the eventual user of the program are translated into a written set of requirements—goals for the product.
2. By assessing feasibility and cost, resolving conflicting requirements, and establishing priorities and tradeoffs, the requirements are translated into specific objectives.
3. The objectives are translated into a precise specification of the product, viewing the product as a black box and considering only its interfaces and interactions with the outside world (e.g., the end user). This description is called the external specification.
4. If the product is a *system* (e.g., operating system, flight-control system, data-base-management system, employee personnel system) rather than a *program* (e.g., compiler, payroll program, text formatter), the next process is one of system design. This step partitions the system into individual programs, components, or subsystems, and defines their interfaces.
5. The program structure of the program(s) is designed by specifying the function of each module, the hierarchial structure of the modules, and the interfaces between modules.
6. A precise specification is developed, specifying the interface to, and function of, each module.
7. Through one or more substeps, the module interface specification is translated into the source-code algorithm of each module.

Looking at these forms of documentation in another way, requirements specify *why* the program is needed, objectives specify *what* the program should do and *how well* the program should do it, external specifications specify the exact *representation* of the program to its users, and the documentation associated with the subsequent processes specifies, in increasing levels of detail, *how* the program is constructed.

Given the premise that these seven steps involve communication, comprehension, and translation of information, and the premise that most software errors stem from breakdowns in information handling, there are three complementary approaches to prevent and/or detect these errors. The first approach is to

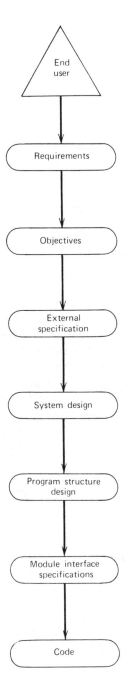

Figure 6.1 **The software development process.**

introduce more precision into the development process so that many of the errors can be prevented. The second approach is to introduce, at the end of each process, a separate verification step having the goal of locating as many errors as possible before proceeding to the next process. This approach is illustrated in Figure 6.2. For instance, the external specification is verified by comparing it to the output of the prior stage (the statement of objectives), feeding back any discovered mistakes to the external-specification process. The code inspection and walkthrough methods discussed in Chapter 3 are used in the verification step at the end of seventh process.

The third approach is to orient distinct testing processes toward distinct development processes, that is, focus each testing process on a particular translation step, thus focusing it on a particular class of errors. This approach is illustrated in Figure 6.3. The testing cycle has been structured to model the development cycle. In other words, one should be able to establish a one-to-one correspondence between development and testing processes. For instance, the purpose of a module test is to find discrepancies between the program's modules and their interface specifications. The purpose of function testing is showing that a program does not match its external specifications. The purpose of system testing is showing that the product is inconsistent with its original objectives. The advantages of this structure are that it avoids unproductive redundant testing and prevents one from overlooking large classes of errors. For instance, rather than simply labeling system testing as "the testing of the whole system" and possibly repeating earlier tests, system testing is oriented toward a distinct class of errors (those made during the translation of the objectives to the external specification) and measured with respect to a distinct type of documentation in the development process.

As noted earlier, the forms of higher-order testing shown in Figure 6.3 are most applicable to software *products* (programs written as a result of a contract or programs intended for wide usage, as opposed to experimental programs or programs written for use only by the program's author). Programs not written as products often do not have formal requirements and objectives; for such programs, the function test might be the only higher-order test. Also, the need for higher-order testing increases as the size of the program increases. The reason is that the ratio of design errors (errors made in the earlier development processes) to coding errors is considerably higher in large programs than in small programs.

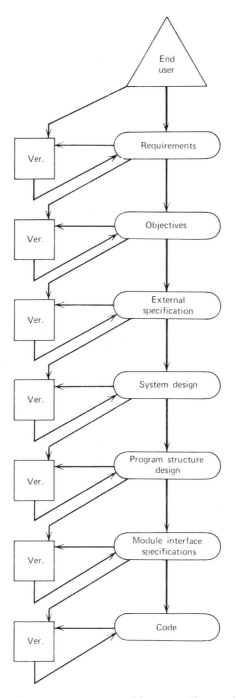

Figure 6.2   **The development process with intermediate verification steps.**

107

Note that the sequence of testing processes in Figure 6.3 does not necessarily imply a time sequence. For instance, since system testing is not defined as "the kind of testing one does after function testing," but is defined as a distinct type of testing focused on a distinct class of errors, it could very well be partially overlapped in time with other testing processes.

In this chapter, the processes of function, system, acceptance, and installation testing are discussed. Integration testing is omitted because it is often not regarded as a separate testing step and, when incremental module testing is used, it is an implicit part of the module test. The discussions of these testing processes will be brief, general, and, for the most part, without examples. The reason is that specific techniques used in these higher-order tests are highly dependent on the specific program being tested. For instance, the characteristics of a system test (e.g., the types of test cases, the manner in which test cases are designed, the test tools used) for an operating system will differ considerably from a system test of a compiler, a program controlling a nuclear reactor, or a data-base application program. The last few sections in the chapter discuss planning and organizational issues and the important question of determining when to stop testing.

FUNCTION TESTING

As indicated in Figure 6.3, function testing is a process of attempting to find discrepancies between the program and its external specification. An external specification is a precise description of the program's behavior from the point of view of the outside world (e.g., its user).

Except when used on small programs, function testing is normally a black-box-oriented activity. That is, one relies on the earlier module-testing process to achieve the desired white-box logic-coverage criteria.

To perform a function test, the specification is analyzed to derive a set of test cases. The equivalence partitioning, boundary-value analysis, cause–effect graphing, and error-guessing methods described in Chapter 4 are especially pertinent to function testing. In fact, the examples in Chapter 4 are examples of function tests. The descriptions of the Fortran DIMENSION statement, the examination-scoring program, and the DISPLAY command are actually examples of external specifications. (Note,

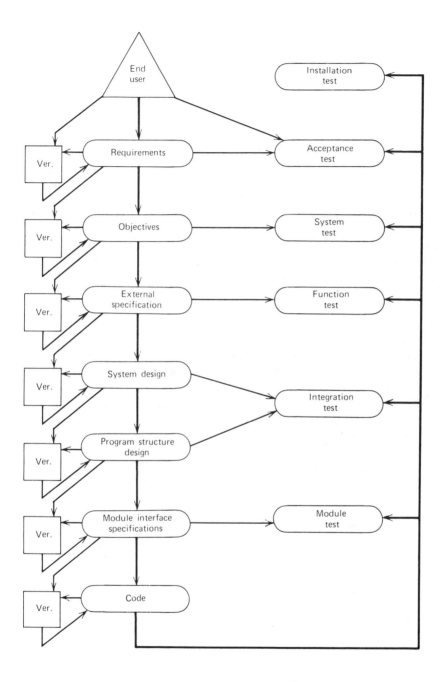

Figure 6.3   **The correspondence between development and testing processes.**

however, that they are not completely realistic examples; for instance, a real external specification for the scoring program would include a precise description of the format of the reports.) Hence no examples of function tests are presented in this section.

Many of the guidelines of Chapter 2 are also particularly pertinent to function testing. Keep track of which functions have exhibited the greatest number of errors; this information is valuable because it tells us that these functions probably also contain the preponderance of as-yet undetected errors. Remember to focus a sufficient amount of attention on invalid and unexpected input conditions. Recall that the definition of the expected result is a vital part of a test case. Finally, as always, remember that the purpose of the function test is to expose errors, not to demonstrate that the program matches its external specification.

SYSTEM TESTING

System testing is both the most misunderstood and most difficult testing process. System testing is not a process of testing the functions of the complete system or program, because this would be redundant with the process of function testing. As shown in Figure 6.3, system testing has a particular purpose: to compare the system or program to its original objectives. Given this purpose, two implications are

1. System testing is not limited to "systems." If the product is a program, system testing is the process of attempting to demonstrate how the program does not meet its objectives.
2. System testing, by definition, is impossible if the project has not produced a written set of measurable objectives for its product.

In looking for discrepancies between the program and its objectives, much of the focus is on translation errors made during the process of designing the external specification. This makes the system test a vital test process, because in terms of the product of the number of errors made and the severity of those errors, this step in the development cycle is usually the most error-prone step. It also implies that, unlike the function test, the external specification cannot be used as the basis for deriving the system test cases, since this would subvert the purpose of the system test. On the other hand, the objectives document cannot be used, by itself, to formulate test cases, since it does not, by definition, contain precise descriptions of the program's external interfaces. This dilemma is solved by using the program's user documentation or publications. System test cases are designed by analyzing the objectives and then formulated by analyzing the user documentation. This has the useful side effect of not only comparing the program to its objectives, but also comparing the program to the user documentation and comparing the user documentation to the objectives, as shown in Figure 6.4.

The reason that system testing is the most difficult testing process is that the leftmost arrow in Figure 6.4, comparing the program to its objectives, is the central purpose of the system test, but there are no known test-case-design methodologies. The reason for this is that objectives state what a program should do, and how well the program should do it, but do not state the representation of the program's functions. For instance, the objec-

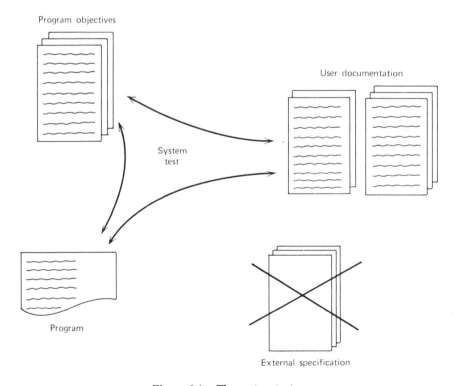

Figure 6.4   The system test.

tives for the DISPLAY command specified in Chapter 4 might have read as follows:

A command will be provided to view, from a terminal, the contents of main-storage locations. Its syntax should be consistent with the syntax of all other system commands. The user should be able to specify a range of locations, both via an address range or an address and a count. Sensible defaults should be provided for command operands.

Output should be displayed as multiple lines of multiple words (in hexadecimal), with spacing between the words. Each line should contain the address of the first word of that line. The command is a "trivial" command, meaning that, under reasonable system loads, it should begin displaying output within two seconds, and there should be no observable delay between output lines. A programming error in the command processor should, at the worst, cause the command to fail; the sytem and the user's session must not be affected. The command processor should have no more than one user-detected error after the system is put into production.

Given this statement of objectives, there is no identifiable methodology that can be applied to it to yield a set of test cases, other than the vague, but useful, guideline of writing test cases to attempt to show that the program is inconsistent with each sentence in the objectives statement. Hence a different approach to test-case design is taken here; rather than describing a methodology, distinct categories of system test cases are discussed. Because of the absence of a methodology, system testing requires a substantial amount of creativity; in fact, the design of good system test cases requires more creativity, intelligence, and experience than that required to design the system or program.

The 15 categories of test cases are discussed below. It is not claimed that all 15 categories will be applicable to every program, but, to avoid overlooking something, all 15 categories should be explored when designing test cases.

Facility Testing

The most obvious type of system testing is the determination of whether each facility (or function, but the word "function" is not used here to avoid confusing this with function testing) mentioned in the objectives was actually implemented. The procedure is to scan the objectives sentence by sentence and, when the sentence specifies a *what* (e.g., "syntax should be consistent. . .," "user should be able to specify a range of locations. . ."), determine if the program satisfies the "what." This type of testing can often be performed without the use of a computer; a mental comparison of the objectives with the user documentation is sometimes sufficient.

Volume Testing

A second type of system testing is subjecting the program to heavy volumes of data. For instance, a compiler would be fed an absurdly large source program to compile. A linkage editor might be fed a program containing thousands of modules. An electronic-circuit simulator would be given a circuit containing thousands of components. An operating system's job queue would be filled to capacity. If a program is supposed to handle files spanning multiple volumes (e.g., tape reels), enough data are created to cause the program to switch from one volume to another. In other words, the purpose of volume testing is to show that the program cannot handle the volume of data specified in its objectives.

Since volume testing being obviously expensive, in terms of both machine and people time, one must not go overboard. However, every program must be exposed to at least a few volume tests.

Stress Testing

Stress testing involves subjecting the program to heavy loads or stresses. This should not be confused with volume testing; a heavy stress is a peak volume of data encountered *over a short span of time*. An analogy is an appraisal of a typist. A volume test is the determination of whether the typist can cope with a draft of a large report; a stress test is the determination of whether the typist can type at a rate of 50 words per minute.

Because stress testing involves an element of time, it is not applicable to many programs, for example, a compiler or a batch-processing payroll program. It is applicable, however, to programs that operate under varying loads, or interactive, real-time, and process-control programs. If an air-traffic-control system is supposed to keep track of up to 200 planes in its sector, it is stress tested by simulating the existence of 200 planes. Since there is nothing to physically keep a 201st plane from entering the sector, a further stress test would explore the system's reaction to this unexpected plane. An additional stress test might simulate the *simultaneous* entry of a large number of planes into the sector.

If an operating system is supposed to support a maximum of 15 multiprogrammed jobs, the system is stressed by attempting to run 15 jobs simultaneously. If a time-sharing system supports up to 64 terminals, subject the system to the extreme pressure of 64 terminal users trying to sign onto the system simultaneously. (This is not a "never will occur" situation; it occurs in real life when such a system crashes during operation and is immediately brought back on the air by its operator.) Stress a pilot-training aircraft simulator by determining the system's reaction to the trainee's forcing the rudder left, pulling back on the throttle, lowering the flaps, lifting the nose, lowering the landing gear, turning on the landing lights, and banking left, all at the same time. (Such a test case might require a four-handed pilot or, more realistically, two test specialists in the cockpit.) A process-control system might be stress tested by causing all of the monitored processes to generate signals simultaneously. A telephone-switching system is subjected to stress tests by routing to it a large number of simultaneous phone calls.

Although many stress tests do represent conditions that the program will likely experience during its operational use, other stress tests may truly represent "never will occur" situations, but this does not imply that these tests are not useful. If errors are detected by these "impossible" conditions, the test is valuable, because it is likely that the same errors might also occur in realistic, less-stressful, situations.

Usability Testing

Another important category of system test cases is an attempt to find human-factor, or usability, problems. Unfortunately, since the computing industry has placed insufficient attention on studying and defining good human-factor considerations of programming systems, an analysis of human factors is still a highly subjective matter. The following is a list illustrating the kinds of considerations that might be tested.

1. Has each user interface been tailored to the intelligence, educational background, and environmental pressures of the end user?

2. Are the outputs of the program meaningful, nonabusive, devoid of "computer gibberish," and so on?

3. Are the error diagnostics (e.g., error messages) straightforward, or does one need need a Ph.D. in computer science to comprehend them? For instance, does the program produce such messages as "IEK022A OPEN ERROR ON FILE 'SYSIN' ABEND CODE=102"?

4. Does the total set of user interfaces exhibit considerable "conceptual integrity" [2], an underlying consistency and uniformity of syntax, conventions, semantics, format, style, and abbreviations?

5. Where accuracy is vital (e.g., in an online banking system), is sufficient redundancy present in the input (e.g., account number *and* customer name)?

6. Does the system contain an excessive number of options, or options that are unlikely to be used?

7. Does the system return some type of immediate acknowledgment to all inputs?

8. Is the program easy to use? For instance, does entering a command into a time-sharing system require repeated shifts between upper- and lower-case characters?

Security Testing

Because of society's increasing concern about privacy, many programs have specific security objectives. Security testing is the process of attempting to devise test cases that subvert the program's security checks. For instance, one tries to formulate test cases that subvert an operating system's memory-protection mechanism. One tries to subvert a data-base-management system's data-security mechanisms. One way to devise such test cases is to study known security problems in similar systems and generate test cases that attempt to demonstrate similar problems in the system at hand. For instance, descriptions exist [3, 4] of known security holes in operating systems.

Performance Testing

Many programs have specific performance or efficiency objectives, stating such properties as response times and throughput rates under certain workload and configuration conditions. Again, since the purpose of a system test is to demonstrate that the program does not meet its objectives, test cases must be devised that attempt to show that the program does not satisfy its performance objectives.

Storage Testing

Similarly, programs occasionally have storage objectives, stating, for instance, the amounts of main and secondary storage used by the program and the sizes of required temporary or spill files. Test cases should be devised to show that these storage objectives have not been met.

Configuration Testing

Such programs as operating systems, data-base management systems, and message-switching programs support a variety of hardware configurations (e.g., types and number of I/O devices and communication lines, different memory sizes). Often the number of possible configurations is too large to attempt to test the program with each one, but, at the least, the program should be tested with each type of hardware device and with the minimum and maximum configuration. If the program itself can be configured (e.g., components of the program can be omitted or placed in separate processors), each possible configuration of the program should be tested.

Compatibility/Conversion Testing

Most programs that are developed are not completely new; they are often replacements for some deficient system, either a data-processing or manual system. As such, programs often have specific objectives concerning their compatibility with, and conversion procedures from, the existing system. Again, in testing the program to these objectives, the orientation of the test cases is to demonstrate that the compatibility objectives have not been met and that the conversion procedures do not work.

Installability Testing

Some types of software systems have complicated procedures for installing the system (e.g., the system generation, or "sysgen," process in IBM's operating systems). The testing of these installation procedures is part of the system-testing process.

Reliability Testing

Of course, the goal of all types of testing is the improvement of the eventual reliability of the program, but, if the program's objectives contain specific statements about reliability, specific reliability tests might be devised. Testing reliability objectives can be difficult. For instance, the Bell System's TSPS switching system has a down-time objective of 2 hours or less per 40 years of operation; there is no known way that one can test this objective given a test period of months or even a few years. However, if the program has mean-time-to-failure objectives (e.g., MTTF = 20 hours) or operational-error objectives (e.g., the program should experience no more than 12 unique errors after it is placed into production), there are a set of mathematical models (see Chapter 8 or reference 1, chapter 18) that allow one to estimate the validity of such objectives.

Recovery Testing

Such programs as operating system, data-base management systems, and teleprocessing programs often have recovery objectives, stating how the system is to recover from programming errors, hardware failures, and data errors. One objective of the system test is to show that these recovery functions do not work correctly. Programming errors can be purposely injected into an operating system to determine if it can recover from them. Hardware failures (e.g., memory parity errors, I/O device errors) can be simulated. Data errors (e.g., noise on a communications line, an invalid pointer in a data base) can be purposely created or simulated to analyze the system's reaction.

Serviceability Testing

The program may also have objectives for its serviceability or maintainability characteristics. All objectives of this sort must be tested. Such objectives might define the service aids to be provided with the system (e.g., storage-dump programs, diagnostic programs), the mean time to debug an apparent problem, the maintenance procedures, and the quality of internal-logic documentation.

Documentation Testing

As was illustrated in Figure 6.4, the system test is also concerned with the accuracy of the user documentation. The principal way of accomplishing this is the use of the user documentation to determine the representation of the prior system test cases (e.g., once a particular stress test is devised, the user documentation is used as a guide for writing the actual test case). Also, the user documentation should be the subject of an inspection (similar to the concept of the code inspection in Chapter 3), checking it for accuracy and clarity. Any examples illustrated in the documentation should be encoded into test cases and fed to the program.

Procedure Testing

Finally, many programs are parts of larger, not completely automated, systems involving procedures performed by people. Any prescribed human procedures, such as procedures to be followed by the system operator, data-base administrator, or terminal user, should be tested during the system test.

Performing the System Test

One of the most vital considerations in implementing the system test is the determination of who should do it. To answer this in a negative way, (1) a system test should not be performed by programmers; and (2) of all the testing phases, this is the one that should *definitely* not be performed by the organization responsible for developing the program.

The first point stems from the fact that a person performing a system test must be capable of thinking like an end user of the program, which implies a thorough understanding of the attitudes and environment of the end user and of how the program will be used. Obviously then, if feasible, a good candidate is one or more end users. However, because the typical end user will not have the ability or expertise to perform many of the categories of tests described earlier, an ideal system-test team might be composed of a few professional system-test experts (people who spend their lives performing system tests), a representative end user or two, a human-factors engineer, and the key original analysts or designers of the program. Including the original designers does not violate the earlier principle recommending against one testing one's own program, since the program has probably passed through many hands since they conceived it. Hence, the original designers do not have the troublesome psychological ties to the program that motivated this principle.

The second point stems from the fact that a system test is an "anything goes, no holds barred" activity. Again, the development organization has psychological ties to the program that are counter to this type of activity. Also, most development organizations are most interested in having the system test proceed as "smoothly" as possible and on schedule, and are not truly motivated to demonstrate that the program does not meet its objectives. At the least, the system test should be performed by an independent group of people, with few, if any, organizational ties to the development organization. Perhaps the most economical way of conducting a system test (economical in terms of finding the most errors with a given amount of money, or spending less money to find the same number of errors) is to subcontract it to a separate company. This is discussed further in the last section of this chapter.

ACCEPTANCE TESTING

Returning to the overall model of the development process in Figure 6.3, one sees that acceptance testing is the process of comparing the program to its initial requirements and the current needs of its end users. It is an unusual type of test in that it is usually performed by the program's customer or end user, and normally is not considered the responsibility of the development organization. In the case of a contracted program, the contracting (user) organization performs the acceptance test by comparing the program's operation to the original contract. As is the case for other types of testing, the best way to do this is to devise test cases attempting to show that the program does not meet the contract; if these test cases are unsuccessful, the program is accepted. In the case of a program product (e.g., a computer manufacturer's operating system or compiler, a software company's data-base system), the sensible customer first performs an acceptance test to determine whether the product satisfies its needs.

INSTALLATION TESTING

The remaining testing process in Figure 6.3 is the installation test. Its position in Figure 6.3 is a bit unusual, since it is not related, as all of the other testing processes are, to specific phases in the design process. It *is* an unusual type of testing, because its purpose is not to find software errors, but to find installation errors.

When installing many software systems, a variety of options must be selected by the user, files and libraries must be allocated and loaded, a valid hardware configuration must be present, and the programs must be interconnected to other programs. The purpose of the installation test is to locate any errors made during this installation process.

Installation tests should be developed by the organization that produced the system, delivered as part of the system, and run after the system is installed. Among other things, the test cases might check to ensure that a compatible set of options has been selected, that all parts of the system exist, that all files have been created and have the necessary contents, and that the hardware configuration is appropriate.

TEST PLANNING AND CONTROL

If one considers that the testing of a large system could entail writing, executing, and verifying tens of thousands of test cases, handling thousands of modules, repairing thousands of errors, and employing perhaps hundreds of people at some time or another over a time span of a year or more, it is apparent that one is faced with an immense project-management problem in planning, monitoring, and controlling the testing process. In fact, the problem is so enormous that one could envision an entire book devoted to just the management of software testing. The intent of this section to summarize some of these considerations.

The major mistake made in planning a testing process has already been mentioned in Chapter 2; it is the tacit assumption made, when planning a schedule, that no errors will be found. The obvious result of this mistake is that the planned resources (people, calendar time, and computer time) will be grossly underestimated, a notorious problem in the computing industry. Compounding the problem is the fact that the testing process falls at the end of the development cycle, meaning that resource changes are difficult. A second, perhaps more significant, problem is that it is a sign that the wrong definition of testing is being used, since it is difficult to see how someone using the correct definition of testing (the goal being to find errors) would plan a test using the assumption that no errors will be found.

As is the case for most undertakings, the plan is the crucial part of the management of the testing process. The components of a good test plan are

1. *Objectives.* The objectives of each testing phase must be defined.
2. *Completion criteria.* Criteria specifying when each testing phase will be judged to be complete must be specified. This matter is discussed in the next section.
3. *Schedules.* Calendar-time schedules are needed for each phase. They should indicate when test cases will be designed, written, and executed.
4. *Responsibilities.* For each phase, the people who will design, write, execute, and verify test cases, and the people who will repair discovered errors, should be identified. Since disputes often unfortunately arise, in large projects, over whether particular test results represent errors (e.g., because of ambiguities or missing definitions in the specifications), an arbitrator should be identified.
5. *Test-case libraries and standards.* In a large project, systematic methods of identifying, writing, and storing test cases are necessary.
6. *Tools.* The required test tools must be identified, including a plan for who will develop or acquire them, how they will be used, and when they are needed.
7. *Computer time.* This is a plan for the amount of computer time needed for each testing phase.
8. *Hardware configuration.* If special hardware configurations or devices are needed, a plan describing the requirements, how they will be met, and when they are needed is necessary.
9. *Integration.* Part of the test plan is a definition of how the program will be pieced together (e.g., incremental top-down testing). A system containing major subsystems or programs might be pieced together incrementally (e.g., using the top-down or bottom-up approach, but where the building blocks are programs or subsystems, rather than modules); if so, a system integration plan is necessary. The system integration plan defines the order of integration, the functional capability of each version of the system, and responsibilities for producing "scaffolding" (code that simulates the function of nonexistent components).
10. *Tracking procedures.* Means must be identified to track various aspects of testing progress, including the location of error-prone modules and estimation of progress with respect to the schedule, resources, and completion criteria.

11. *Debugging procedures.* Mechanisms must be defined for reporting detected errors, tracking the progress of corrections, and adding the corrections to the system. Schedules, responsibilities, tools, and computer time must also be part of the debugging plan.

12. *Regression testing.* Regression testing is that testing that is performed after making a functional improvement or repair to the program. Its purpose is to determine if the change has regressed other aspects of the program. It is usually performed by rerunning some subset of the program's test cases. Regression testing is important because changes and error corrections tend to be much more error prone than the original code in the program (in much the same way that most typographical errors in newspapers are the result of last-minute editorial changes, rather than errors in the original copy). A plan for regression testing (e.g., who, how, when) is another necessity.

TEST COMPLETION CRITERIA

One of the most difficult questions to answer when testing a program is determining when to stop, since there is no way of knowing if the error just detected is the last remaining error. In fact, in anything but a small program, it is unreasonable to expect that all errors will eventually be detected. Given this dilemma, and given the fact that economics dictate that testing must eventually terminate, one might wonder if the question has to be answered in a purely arbitrary way, or if there are some useful stopping criteria.

The completion criteria typically used in practice are both meaningless and counterproductive. The two most common criteria are

1. Stop when the scheduled time for testing expires.
2. Stop when all the test cases execute without detecting errors (i.e., when the test cases are unsuccessful).

The first criterion is useless because it can be satisfied by doing absolutely nothing (i.e., it does not measure the quality of the testing). The second criterion is equally useless because it also is independent of the quality of the test cases. Furthermore, it is counterproductive because it subconsciously encourages one to write test cases that have a low probability of detecting errors.

As discussed in Chapter 2, human beings are highly goal-oriented; if one is told that he has finished a task when his test cases are unsuccessful, he will subconsciously write test cases that lead him to this goal, avoiding the useful, high-yield, destructive test cases.

There are three categories of more-useful criteria. The first category, but not the best, is to base completion on the use of specific test-case-design methodologies. For instance, one might define the completion of module testing as the following:

The test cases are derived from (1) satisfying the multicondition-coverage criterion and (2) a boundary-value analysis of the module interface specification, and all resultant test cases are eventually unsuccessful.

One might define the function test as being complete when the following conditions are satisfied:

The test cases are derived from (1) cause–effect graphing, (2) boundary-value analysis, and (3) error guessing, and all resultant test cases are eventually unsuccessful.

Although this type of criterion is superior to the two mentioned earlier, it has three problems. First, it is not helpful in a test phase in which specific methodologies are not available, such as the system-test phase. Second, it is a subjective measurement, since there is no way to guarantee that a person has used a particular methodology (e.g., boundary-value analysis) properly and rigorously. Third, rather than giving one a goal and letting him choose the most appropriate way of achieving it, it does the opposite; the test-case-design methodologies are dictated, but no goal is given. Hence this type of criterion is useful sometimes for *some* testing phases, but it should only be applied when the tester has proven his or her abilities in the past in applying the test-case-design methodologies successfully.

The second category of criteria, perhaps the most valuable one, is to state the completion requirements in *positive* terms. Since the goal of testing is to find errors, why not make the completion criterion be the detection of some predefined number of errors? For instance, one might state that a module test of a particular module is not complete until 3 errors are discovered. Perhaps the completion criterion for a system test should be defined as the detection and repair of 70 errors or an elapsed time of 3 months, whichever comes later.

Notice that this type of criterion reinforces the definition of

testing. It does have two problems, both of which are surmounta-
ble. One problem is determing how to obtain the number of errors
to be detected. Obtaining this number requires

1. An estimate of the total number of errors in the program.
2. An estimate of what percentage of these errors can be feasi-
    bly found through testing.
3. Estimates of what fraction of the errors originated in partic-
    ular design processes, and during what testing phases these
    errors are likely to be detected.

A rough estimate of the total number of errors can be obtained in several ways. One method is obtaining them through
experience with previous programs. Also, a variety of predictive
models exist (e.g., reference 1, chapter 18). Some of these models
require one to test the program for some period of time, record
the elapsed times between the detection of successive errors, and
insert these times into parameters in a formula. Other models
involve the seeding of known, but unpublicized, errors into the
program, testing the program for a while, and then examining
the ratio of detected seeded errors to detected unseeded errors.
Another model employs two independent test teams who test for
a while, examine the errors found by each and the errors detected in common by both teams, and use these parameters to
estimate the total number of errors. Another gross method to
obtain this estimate is to use industry-wide averages. For instance, the number of errors that exist in typical programs at the
time that coding is completed (before a code walkthrough or inspection is employed) is approximately 4–8 errors per 100 program statements.

Estimate 2 (the percentage of errors that can be feasibly
found through testing) involves a somewhat arbitrary guess,
taking into consideration the nature of the program and the consequences of undetected errors.

Given the current paucity of information about how and when
errors are made, estimate 3 is the most difficult. The data that
exist indicate that, in large programs, approximately 40% of the
errors are coding and logic-design mistakes, and the remainder
are generated in the earlier design processes.

Although the reader, to use this criterion, must develop his or
her own estimates that are pertinent to the program at hand, a
simple example is presented here. Assume we are about to begin
testing a 10,000-statement program, the number of errors re-

maining after code inspections are performed is estimated at five per 100 statements, and we establish, as an objective, the detection of 98% of the coding and logic-design errors and 95% of the design errors. The total number of errors is thus estimated as 500. Of the 500 errors, we assume that 200 are coding and logic-design errors, and 300 are design flaws. Hence the goal is to find 196 coding and logic-design errors and 285 design errors. A plausible estimate of when the errors are likely to be detected is shown in Table 6.1.

If we have scheduled four months for function testing and three months for system testing, the completion criteria might be established as

1. Module testing is complete when 130 errors are found and corrected (65% of the estimated 200 coding and logic-design errors).
2. Function testing is complete when 240 errors (30% of 200 plus 60% of 300) are found and corrected, or when four months of function testing have expired, whichever occurs later. (The reason for the second clause is that if we find 240 errors quickly, this is probably an indication that we have underestimated the total number of errors and thus should not stop function testing early.)
3. System testing is complete when 111 errors are found and corrected, or when three months of system testing have expired, whichever occurs later.

The other obvious problem with this type of criterion is one of overestimation. What if, in the above example, there are less than 240 errors remaining when function test starts? Based on the criterion, we could never complete the function-test phase.

Table 6.1   Hypothetical Estimate of When the Errors Might Be Found

	Coding and logic-design errors	Design errors
Module test	65%	0%
Function test	30%	60%
System test	3%	35%
Total	98%	95%

This is a strange problem if one thinks about it. Our "problem" is that we do not have enough errors; the program is too good. One could label it a nonproblem because it is the kind of problem that a lot of people would love to have. If it does occur, a bit of common sense can solve it. If we cannot find 240 errors in four months, the project manager can employ an outsider to analyze the test cases to judge whether the problem is (1) inadequate test cases or (2) excellent test cases but a lack of errors to detect.

The third type of completion criterion is an easy one on the surface, but it involves a lot of judgment and intuition. It requires one to plot the number of errors found per unit time during the test phase. By examining the shape of the curve, one can often determine whether to continue the test phase or end it and begin the next test phase.

Suppose a program is being function tested and the number of errors found per week is being plotted. If, in the seventh week, the curve is the left one of Figure 6.5, it would be imprudent to stop the function test, even if we had reached our criterion for the number of errors to be found. Since, in the seventh week, we still seem to be in high gear (finding many errors), the wisest decision (remembering that our goal is to find errors) is to continue function testing, designing additional test cases if necessary.

On the other hand, suppose the curve is the right one in Figure 6.5. The error-detection efficiency has dropped significantly, implying that we have perhaps picked the function-test bone clean and that perhaps the best move is to terminate function testing and begin a new type of testing (e.g., system test). (Of course, we must also consider other factors such as whether the

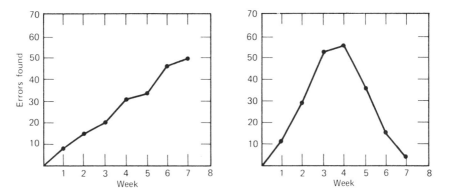

Figure 6.5   Estimating completion by plotting errors detected per unit time.

drop in error-detection efficiency was due to a lack of computer time or exhaustion of the available test cases.)

Figure 6.6 is an illustration of what happens when one fails to plot the number of errors being detected. The graph represents three testing phases of an extremely large software system [5]; it was drawn as part of a post-mortem study of the project. An obvious conclusion is that the project should not have switched to a different testing phase after period 6. During period 6, the error-detection rate was good (to a tester, the higher the rate, the better), but switching to a second phase at this point caused the error-detection rate to drop significantly.

The best completion criterion is probably a combination of the three types discussed above. For the module test, particularly because most projects do not formally track detected errors during this phase, the best completion criterion is probably the first; one should request that a particular set of test-case-design methodologies be used. For the function- and system-test phases, the completion rule might be to stop when a predefined number of

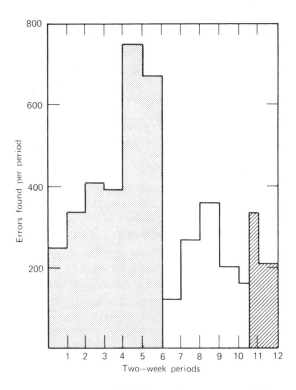

Figure 6.6 Post–mortem study of the testing processes of a large project.

errors are detected, or when the scheduled time has elapsed, whichever comes later, but provided that an analysis of the errors-versus-time graph indicates that the test has become unproductive.

THE INDEPENDENT TEST AGENCY

Earlier in the chapter, and in Chapter 2, it was emphasized that an organization should avoid attempting to test its own programs. The reasoning was that the organization responsible for developing a program has difficulty in objectively testing the same program. The test organization should be as far removed as possible, in terms of the structure of the company, from the development organization. In fact it is desirable that the test organization not be part of the same company, for if it is, it is still influenced by the same management pressures influencing the development organization.

As an indication of what might be done, suggestions have been made within the U.S. Air Force that, when a contract is written with an outside company for the development of software, a separate contract be written with a different company for the testing of that software [6]. The Air Force now has its own, organizationally separate, testing organization (the Air Force Test and Evaluation Center), and has recently used outside testing contractors who are independent from the prime contractor [7].

Apparently, this step has been effective, as is indicated by the following statement [8]:

> One of the most successful approaches to improving software reliability that the Air Force has used to date, particularly on highly critical real-time software, is the utilization of an independent software agency to perform analysis, testing, and overall evaluation.

The advantages usually noted are increased motivation in the testing process, a healthy competition with the development organization, removal of the testing process from under the management control of the development organization, and the advantages of specialized knowledge that the independent test agency bring to bear on the problem. If this attitude catches on, it presents opportunities for entrepreneurs interested in starting a unique type of data-processing business.

REFERENCES

1. G. J. Myers, *Software Reliability: Principles and Practices*. New York: Wiley–Interscience, 1976.

2. F. P. Brooks, Jr., *The Mythical Man-Month: Essays on Software Engineering*. Reading, Mass.: Addison-Wesley, 1975.

3. W. S. McPhee, "Operating System Integrity in OS/VS2," *IBM Systems J.* **13** (3), 230–252 (1974).

4. P. L. Pinchuk, "TRW Evaluation of a Secure Operating System," *Data Security and Data Processing, Volume 6, Evaluation and Installation Experiences: Resource Security System*. White Plains, N.Y.: IBM, 1974, G320-1376.

5. C. R. Craig et al., "Software Reliability Study," RADC-TR-74-250, TRW Corp., Redundo Beach, Cal., 1974.

6. M. Shelley, "Computer Software Reliability: Fact or Myth?" TR-MMER/RM-73-125, Hill Air Force Base, Utah, 1973.

7. C. R. Magill, "The Role of an Independent Software Validation Agency," Report 76-1, Defense Systems Management School, Fort Belvoir, Va., 1976

8. R. H. Thayer and E. S. Hinton, "Software Reliability—A Method that Works," *Proceedings of the 1975 National Computer Conference*. Montvale, N.J.: AFIPS Press, 1975, pp. 877–883.

CHAPTER 7

Debugging

Based on earlier definitions in the book, the process of program debugging can be described as the activity that one performs after executing a successful test case. Describing it in more concrete terms, debugging is a two-part process; it begins with some indication of the existence of an error (e.g., the results of a successful test case), and it is the activity of (1) determining the exact nature and location of the suspected error within the program and (2) fixing or repairing the error.

Debugging appears to be the single part of the software-production process that programmers seem to abhor the most. The reasons for this attitude appear to be

1. People who do not practice "egoless programming" [1] often find it to be psychologically difficult, because it is an indication that they are less than perfect (i.e., they have made an error when designing and coding the program).

2. Of all the software-development activities, it is the most mentally taxing ac-

tivity. Moreover, the fact that debugging is usually performed under a tremendous amount of pressure (either organizational or self-induced pressure to fix the suspected error as quickly as possible) compounds the problem.

3. One reason for debugging being a mentally taxing process is that, because of the way in which most programs are designed and because of the nature of most programming languages, the location of any error is potentially any statement in the program. That is, without examining the program first, we cannot theoretically eliminate the possibility that a numerical error in a paycheck produced by a payroll program is located in a subroutine that asks the system operator to load a particular form into the printer. Contrast this with the debugging of a physical system, such as an automobile. If a car appears to stall when moving up an incline (the symptom), one can immediately and validly eliminate parts of the system as being the cause (e.g., the AM/FM radio, the speedometer, the trunk lock). The problem must be in the engine, and, based on our overall knowledge of automotive engines, we can rule out certain engine components such as the water pump and the oil filter.

4. Compared to the other software-development activities, comparatively little research, literature, and formal instruction exist on the process of debugging.

Although this is a book about testing, not debugging, a brief discussion of the debugging process is warranted, since the two are obviously related. Of the two aspects of debugging (locating the error and correcting it), the first represents perhaps 95% of the problem. Hence, this chapter concentrates on the process of finding the location of an error, given a suspicion that an error exists (i.e., based on the results of a test case).

DEBUGGING BY BRUTE FORCE

The most common method of program debugging is the rather inefficient "brute force" method. Perhaps the reason for its popularity is that it requires little thought and is the least mentally taxing of the methods, but it is usually the most inefficient and unsuccessful method.

The brute-force methods can be partitioned into at least three categories: (1) debugging with a storage dump, (2) debugging according to the common suggestion to "scatter print statements throughout your program," and (3) debugging with automated debugging tools. Debugging by analyzing a storage dump (usually a crude display of all storage locations in octal or hexadecimal format) is probably the most inefficient method. The problems are

1. The difficulty of establishing the correspondence between storage locations and the variables in one's source program.
2. The massive amount of data with which one is faced, most of which is irrelevant.
3. The fact that a dump is a *static* picture of the program (i.e., it shows the state of the program at only one instant in time), but, to find most errors, one must study the *dynamics* of the program (i.e., state changes over time).
4. The fact that the dump is rarely produced at the exact point of the error. Hence the dump does not show the program's state at the point of the error; actions taken by the program between the time of the error and the time of the dump can mask the required clues.
5. The lack of describable methodologies for finding the cause of an error by analyzing a storage dump (which leads to many programmers staring, with glazed eyes, at the dump, wistfully expecting the error to expose itself magically).

Category 2, scattering statements throughout a failing program to display the values of variables, is not much better. Although it is often superior to the use of a dump in that it displays the dynamics of a program and allows one to examine information that is easier to relate to the source program, it exhibits many shortcomings. Some of these are

1. Rather than encouraging one to *think* about the problem being debugged, it is largely a hit-or-miss method.
2. It can result in a massive amount of data to be analyzed.
3. It requires one to change the program; such changes can mask the error, alter critical timing relationships, or introduce new errors into the program.
4. Although it may be used on small programs, the cost of using it on large programs or systems may be immense. Furthermore, it is often infeasible on certain types of programs (e.g., operating systems, process-control programs).

Category 3, the use of automated debugging tools, is similar to category 2, but rather than inserting changes into the program, one analyzes the dynamics of the program by using debugging features of the programming language or special interactive debugging tools. Typical language features that might be used are facilities that produce printed traces of statement executions, subroutine calls, and/or alterations of specified variables. A common function of debugging tools is the ability to set "breakpoints," causing the program to be suspended when a particular statement is executed or a particular variable is altered, and allowing the programmer at the terminal to examine the current state of the program. Again, this method is largely a hit-or-miss method and often results in an excessive amount of irrelevant data.

The general problem with these brute-force methods is that they ignore the process of *thinking*. One can draw an analogy between program debugging and solving a homicide. In virtually all murder mystery novels, the mystery is solved by careful analyses of the clues and the piecing together of seemingly insignificant details, rather than by brute-force methods such as roadblocks and property searches. As evidence that this happens in real life, the suspect in the New York ".44-caliber killings" in 1976–1977 was not located by the attempted brute-force approaches of saturating the airways and newspapers with artists' drawings of the suspect and deploying large numbers of police on the streets; the suspect was apprehended by discovering several small clues, one being a parking ticket.

There is also experimental evidence [2,3], both from students and experienced programmers, showing that debugging aids do not assist the debugging process, and that, in terms of the speed and accuracy of finding the error, people who use their brains rather than a set of "aids" seem to exhibit superior performance. Hence, the use of brute-force methods is recommended only (1) when all other methods fail or (2) as a supplement to (not a substitute for) the thought processes described in the subsequent sections.

DEBUGGING BY INDUCTION

It is the contention, then, that most errors can be located by careful thought, in many cases without ever going near the com-

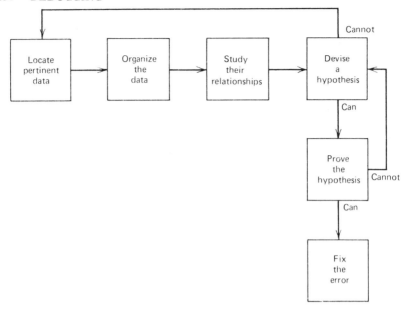

Figure 7.1   **The inductive debugging process.**

puter. One such thought process is induction, where one proceeds from the particulars to the whole. That is, by starting with the clues (the symptoms of the error, possibly in the results of one or more test cases) and looking for relationships among the clues, one can often be led to the error.

The induction process is illustrated in Figure 7.1.

The steps are

1. *Locate the pertinent data.* A major mistake made when debugging a program is failing to take account of all available data or symptoms about the problem. The first step is the enumeration of all that is known about what the program did correctly, and what it did incorrectly (i.e., the symptoms that led one to believe that an error exists). Additional valuable clues are provided by similar, but different, test cases that *do not* cause the symptoms to appear.

2. *Organize the data.* Remembering that induction implies that one is progressing from the particulars to the general, the second step is the structuring of the pertinent data to allow one to observe patterns. Of particular importance is the search for *contradictions* (i.e., "the error occurs only when the customer has no outstanding balance in his margin account").

?	Is	Is not
What		
Where		
When		
To what extent		

Figure 7.2   **A method for structuring the clues.**

A particularly useful organizational technique is known as "The Method" [4]. The form shown in Figure 7.2 is used to structure the available data. The "what" boxes list the general symptoms, the "where" boxes describe where the symptoms were observed, the "when" boxes list anything that is known about the times that the symptoms occur, and the "to what extent" boxes describe the scope and magnitude of the symptoms. Notice the "is" and "is not" colulmns; they describe the contradictions that may eventually lead to a hypothesis about the error.

3. *Devise a hypothesis.* The next steps are to study the relationships among the clues and devise, using the patterns that might be visible in the structure of the clues, one or more hypotheses about the cause of the error. If one cannot devise a theory, more data are necessary, possibly obtained by devising and executing additional test cases. If multiple theories seem possible, the most probable one is selected first.

4. *Prove the hypothesis.* A major mistake at this point, given the pressures under which debugging is usually performed, is skipping this step by jumping to conclusions and attempting to fix the problem. However, it is vital to prove the reasonableness of the hypothesis before proceeding. A failure to do this often results in the fixing of only a symptom of the problem, or only a portion of the problem. The hypothesis is proved by comparing it to the original clues or data, making sure that this hypothesis *completely* explains the existence of the clues. If it does not, either the hypothesis is invalid, the hypothesis is incomplete, or multiple errors are present.

?	Is	Is not
What	The median printed in report 3 is incorrect.	The calculation of the mean or standard deviation.
Where	Only on report 3.	On the other reports. The students' grades seem to be calculated correctly.
When	Occurred in a test run using 51 students.	Did not occur in the test runs for 2 and 200 students.
To what extent	The median printed was 26. It also occurred in the test run using one student; the median printed in this case was 1!	

Figure 7.3   **An example of clue structuring.**

As a simple example, assume that an apparent error has been reported in the examination-grading program described in Chapter 4. The apparent error is that the median grade seems incorrect in some, but not all, instances. In a particular test case, 51 students were graded. The mean score was correctly printed as 73.2, but the median printed was 26 instead of the expected value of 82. By examining the results of this test case and a few other test cases, the clues are organized as shown in Figure 7.3.

The next step is to derive a hypothesis about the error, doing so by looking for patterns and contradictions. One contradiction we see is that the error only seems to occur in test cases employing an *odd* number of students. This might be a coincidence, but it seems significant, since one computes a median differently depending on whether there are an even or odd number of samples. One also sees a strange pattern in that, in such test cases, the calculated median is always less than or equal to the number of students ($26 \leq 51$ and $1 \leq 1$). One possible avenue at this point is to run the 51-student test case again, giving the students different grades from before to see how this affects the median calculation. If we do so, the median is still 26: thus the "is not—to what extent" box could be filled in to state "the median seems to be independent of the actual grades." Although this result provides a valuable clue, we might have been able to surmise the error without it. From the data available, the calculated median ap-

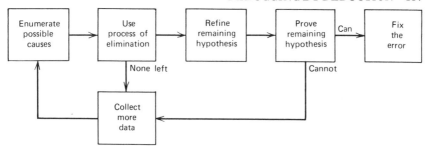

Figure 7.4 The deductive debugging process.

pears to equal half of the number of students, rounded up to the next integer. In other words, if one thinks of the grades as being stored in a sorted table, the program is printing the entry number of the middle student rather than his grade. Hence we have a firm hypothesis about the precise nature of the error. The hypothesis should then be proved by examining the code or running a few extra test cases.

DEBUGGING BY DEDUCTION

The process of deduction, illustrated in Figure 7.4, is a process of proceeding from some general theories or premises, using the processes of elimination and refinement, to arrive at a conclusion (the location of the error). As opposed to the process of induction in a murder case, for example, where one induces a suspect from the clues, one starts with a set of suspects and, by the processes of elimination (the gardener has a valid alibi) and refinement (it must be someone with red hair), decides that the butler must have done it. The steps are

1. *Enumerate the possible causes or hypotheses.* The first step is to devlop a list of all conceivable causes of the error. They need not be complete explanations; they are merely theories through which one can structure and analyze the availabel data.
2. *Use the data to eliminate possible causes.* By a careful analysis of the data, particularly by looking for contradictions (Figure 7.2 could be used here), one attempts to eliminate all but one of the possible causes. If all are eliminated, additional data are needed (e.g., by devising additional test cases) to devise new theories. If more than one possible cause re-

Test–case input	Expected output	Actual output
DISPLAY .E	000000 = 0000 4444 8888 CCCC	M1 INVALID COMMAND SYNTAX
DISPLAY 21–29	000020 = 0000 4444 8888 CCCC	000020 = 4444 8888 CCCC 0000
DISPLAY .11	000000 = 0000 4444 8888 CCCC 000010 = 0000 4444 8888 CCCC	000000 = 0000 4444 8888 CCCC
DISPLAY 8000–END	M2 STORAGE REQUESTED IS BEYOND ACTUAL STORAGE LIMITS	008000 = 0000 4444 8888 CCCC

Figure 7.5   **Test–case results from the DISPLAY command.**

mains, the most probable cause, the prime hypothesis, is selected first.

3. *Refine the remaining hypothesis.* The possible cause at this
point might be correct, but it is unlikely to be specific enough
to pinpoint the error. Hence, the next step is to use the available clues to refine the theory (e.g., "error in handling the
last transaction in the file") to something more specific (e.g.,
"the last transaction in the buffer is overlaid with the end-of-
file indicator").

4. *Prove the remaining hypothesis.* This vital step is identical to
step 4 in the induction method.

As an example, assume that we are commencing the function
testing of the DISPLAY command discussed in Chapter 4. Of the
38 test cases identified by the process of cause–effect graphing,
we start by running 4 test cases. As part of the process of establishing input conditions, storage is initialized so that the first,
fifth, ninth, ..., words have the value 0000, the second, sixth, ...,
words have the value 4444, the third, seventh, ... words have the
value 8888, and the fourth, eighth, ..., words have the value
CCCC. That is, each storage word is initialized to the low order
hexadecimal digit in the address of the first byte of the word (e.g.,
the values of locations 23FC, 23FD, 23FE, and 23FF are C).

The test cases, their expected output, and the actual output
after the test are shown in Figure 7.5. Obviously we have some
problems, since none of the test cases apparently produced the
expected result (all were "successful"), but let us start by debugging the error associated with the first test case. The command
indicates that, starting at location 0 (the default), *E* locations (14
in decimal) are to be displayed. (Recall that the specification
stated that all output will contain 4 words or 16 bytes per line.)

Enumerating the possible causes for the unexpected error message, we might get

1. The program does not accept the word DISPLAY.
2. The program does not accept the period.
3. The program does not allow a default as a first operand (i.e., it expects a storage address to precede the period).
4. The program does not allow an *E* as a valid byte count.

The next step is to attempt to eliminate the causes. If all are eliminated, we must retreat and expand the list. If more than one remain, we might wish to examine additional test cases to arrive at a single error hypothesis, or proceed with the most-probable cause. Since we have other test cases at hand, we see that the second test case in Figure 7.5 seems to eliminate the first hypothesis, and the third test case, although it produced an incorrect result, seems to eliminate the second and third hypotheses.

The next step is to refine the fourth hypothesis. It seems specific enough, but intuition might tell us that there is more to it than meets the eye; it sounds like an instance of a more general error. We might contend, then, that the program does not recognize the special hexadecimal characters (A–F). The absence of such characters in the other test cases makes this sound like a viable explanation.

Rather than jumping to a conclusion, however, we should first consider *all* of the available information. The fourth test case might represent a totally different error, or it might provide a clue about the current error. Given that the highest valid address in our system is 7FFF, how could the fourth test case be displaying an area that appears to be nonexistent? The fact that the displayed values are our initialized values and not garbage might lead to the supposition that this command is somehow displaying something in the range 0–7FFF. One idea that may arise is that this could occur if the program is treating the operands in the command as *decimal* values (rather than hexadecimal, as stated in the specification). This is borne out by the third test case; rather than displaying 32 bytes of storage, the next increment above 11 in hexadecimal (17 in base 10), it displays 16 bytes of storage, which is consistent with our hypothesis that the "11" is being treated as a base–10 value. Hence the refined hypothesis is that the program is treating the byte-count and storage-address operands, and the storage addresses on the output listing, as decimal values.

The last step is to prove this hypothesis. Looking at the fourth test case, if 8000 is interpreted as a decimal number, the corresponding base-16 value is 1F40, which would lead to the output shown. As further proof, examine the second test case. The output is incorrect, but if 21 and 29 are treated as decimal numbers, the locations of storage addresses 15–1D would be displayed; this is consistent with the erroneous result of the test case. Hence we have almost certainly located the error; the program is assuming that the operands are decimal values and is printing the storage addresses as decimal values, which is inconsistent with the specification. Moreover, this error seems to be the cause of the erroneous results of all four test cases. Hence, a little thought has led us to the error, and it has also solved three other problems that, at first glance, appear to be unrelated.

Note that the error probably manifests itself at two locations in the program: the part of the program that interprets the input command, and the part of the program that prints storage addresses on the output listing.

As an aside, this error, likely caused by a misunderstanding of the specification, reinforces the suggestion that a programmer should not attempt to test his or her own program. If the programmer who created this error is also designing the test cases, he or she is likely to make the same mistake while writing the test cases. In other words, the programmer's expected outputs would not be those shown in Figure 7.5; they would be the outputs calculated under the assumption that the operands are decimal values. Hence, this fundamental error would probably go unnoticed.

DEBUGGING BY BACKTRACKING

An effective error-locating method for small programs is to backtrack the incorrect results through the logic of the program until one discovers the point where the logic went astray. In other words, one starts at the point in the program where the incorrect result was produced (e.g., printed); at this point, one deduces, from the observed output, what the values of the program's variables must have been. By performing a mental reverse execution of the program from this point, and repeatedly using the process of "if this was the state of the program (i.e., the values of variables) at this point, then this must have been the state of the program up here," one can often quickly pinpoint the error (i.e., the location in the program between the point where the state of the program was what was expected and the first point where the state was what was not expected).

DEBUGGING BY TESTING

The last "thinking-type" debugging method is the use of test cases. This method sounds, perhaps, a bit peculiar because the beginning of the chapter distinguishes debugging from testing. However, consider two types of test cases: test cases for testing, where the purpose of the test cases is to expose a previously undetected error, and test cases for debugging, where the purpose of the test cases is to provide information useful in locating a suspected error. The difference between the two is that test cases for testing tend to be "fat" (one attempts to cover many conditions in a small number of test cases), but test cases for debugging are "slim" (one attempts to cover only a single condition or a few conditions in each test case).

In other words, after a symptom of a suspected error is discovered, one uses this method by writing variants of the original test case to attempt to pinpoint the error. Actually, this method is not an entirely separate method; one often uses it in conjunction with the induction method (to obtain information needed to generate a hypothesis and/or to prove a hypothesis) or with the deduction method (to eliminate suspected causes, refine the remaining hypothesis, and/or prove a hypothesis).

DEBUGGING PRINCIPLES

Similar to what was done in Chapter 2, a set of debugging principles, many of which are psychological in nature, is discussed in this section. As was the case for the testing principles in Chapter 2, many of these debugging principles are intuitively obvious, yet they are often forgotten or overlooked. Since debugging is a two-part process (locating the error and then repairing it), two sets of principles are presented.

Error-Locating Principles

Think.

As implied in the previous section, debugging is a problem-solving process. The most effective method of debugging is a mental analysis of the information associated with the error's symptoms. An efficient program debugger should be able to pinpoint most errors without going near a computer.

If you reach an impasse, sleep on it.

The human subconsciousness is a potent problem-solver. What we often refer to as inspiration is simply the subconscious mind working on a problem when the conscious mind is working on something else, such as eating, walking, or watching a movie. If you cannot locate an error in a reasonable amount of time (perhaps 30 minutes for a small program, a few hours for a large one), drop it and work on something else, since your thinking efficiency is about to collapse anyway. After "forgetting" about the problem for a while, either your subconscious mind will have solved the problem, or your conscious mind will be clear for a fresh examination of the symptoms.

If you reach an impasse, describe the problem to someone else.

By doing so, you will probably discover something new. In fact, it is often the case that by simply describing the problem to a good listener, you will suddenly see the solution without any assistance from the listener.

Use debugging tools only as a second resort.

And then, use them as an adjunct to, rather than as a substitute for, thinking. As noted earlier in the chapter, debugging tools, such as dumps and traces, represent a haphazard approach to debugging. Experiments show that people who shun such tools, even when they are debugging programs that are unfamiliar to them, tend to be more successful than people who use the tools [3].

Avoid experimentation. Use it only as a last resort.

The most common mistake made by novice debuggers is attempting to solve a problem by making experimental changes to the program (e.g., "I don't know what is wrong, so I'll change this DO statement and see what happens"). This totally haphazard approach cannot even be considered debugging; it represents an act of blind hope. Not only does it have a miniscule chance of success, but it often compounds the problem by adding new errors to the program.

Error-Repairing Principles

Where there is one bug, there is likely to be another.

This is a restatement of the principle in Chapter 2 stating that when one finds an error in a section of a program, the probability of the existence of another error in that section is higher. In other words, errors tend to cluster. When repairing an error, examine its immediate vicinity for anything else that looks suspicious.

Fix the error, not just a symptom of it.

Another common failing is repairing the symptoms of the error, or just one instance of the error, rather than the error itself. If the proposed correction does not match *all* the clues about the error, one may be fixing only a part of the error.

The probability of the fix being correct is not 100%.

Tell this to someone, and of course he would agree, but tell it to someone in the process of correcting an error, and one often gets a different reaction (e.g., "Yes, in most cases, but *this* correction is so minor that it just has to work"). Code that is added to a program to fix an error can never be assumed to be correct. Statement for statement, corrections are much more error prone than the original code in the program. One implication is that error corrections must be tested, perhaps more rigorously than the original program.

The probability of the fix being correct drops as the size of the program increases.

Stating it differently, experience has shown that the ratio of errors due to incorrect fixes versus original errors increases in large programs. In one widely used large program, one of every six new errors discovered is an error in a prior correction to the program.

Beware of the possibility that an error correction creates a new error.

Not only does one have to worry about incorrect corrections, but one has to worry about a seemingly valid correction having an undesirable side effect, thus introducing a new error. Not only is there a probability that a fix will be invalid, but there is also a nonzero probability that a fix will introduce a new error. One implication is that not only does the error situation have to be tested after the correction is made, but one must also perform regression testing to determine if a new error has been introduced.

The process of error repair should put one back temporarily in the design phase.

One should realize that error correction is a form of program design. Given the error-prone nature of corrections, common sense says that whatever procedures, methodologies, and formalism were used in the design process should also apply to the error-correction process. For instance, if the project rationalized that code inspections were desirable, then it must be doubly important that they be used after correcting an error.

Change the source code, not the object code.

When debugging large systems, particularly a system written in an assembly language, occasionally there is the tendency to correct an error by making an immediate change to the object code (i.e., by using a "superzap" program), with the intention of changing the source program later (i.e., "when I have time"). Two problems associated with this approach are (1) it is usually a sign that "debugging by experimentation" is being practiced, and (2) the object code and source program are now out of synchronization, meaning that the error could easily surface again when the program is recompiled or reassembled. This practice is an indication of a sloppy, unprofessional approach to debugging.

ERROR ANALYSIS

The last thing to realize about program debugging is that, in addition to its value in removing an error from the program, it can have another valuable effect: it can tell us something about the nature of software errors, something we still know too little about. Information about the nature of software errors can provide valuable feedback in terms of improving future design and testing processes.

Every programmer and programming organization could improve immensely by performing a detailed analysis of the detected errors, or at least a subset of them. It is a difficult and time-consuming task, for it implies much more than a superficial grouping such as "*X*% of the errors are logic-design errors" or "*Y*% of the errors occur in IF statements." A careful analysis might include the following studies:

1. *When was the error made?* This question is the most difficult one to answer, because it requires a backward search through the documentation and history of the project, but it is also the most valuable question. It requires one to pinpoint the *original* source and time of the error. For example, the original source of the error might be discovered to be an ambiguous statement in a specification, a correction to a prior error, or a misunderstanding of an end-user requirement.

2. *Who made the error?* Wouldn't it be useful to discover that 60% of the design errors were created by 1 of the 10 analysts, or that programmer *X* makes three times as many mistakes as the other programmers? (Not for purposes of punishment, but for purposes of education.)

3. *What was done incorrectly?* It is not sufficient to determine when and by whom each error was made; the missing link is a determination of exactly why the error occurred. Was it caused by someone's inability to write clearly? Someone's lack of education in the programming language? A typing or keypunching mistake? An invalid assumption? A failure to consider invalid input?

4. *How could the error have been prevented?* What can be done differently in the next project to prevent this type of error? The answer to this question is much of the valuable feedback or learning for which we are searching.

5. *Why wasn't the error detected earlier?* If the error is detected during a test phase, one should study why the error was not detected during earlier testing phases, code inspections, and design reviews.

6. *How could the error have been detected earlier?* The answer to this is another piece of valuable feedback. How can the review and testing processes be improve to find this type of error earlier in future projects?

7. *How was the error found?* Providing that we are not analyzing an error found by an end user (i.e., the error was found by a test case), we should realize that something valuable has happened: we have written a successful test case. Why was this test case successful? Can we learn something from it that will result in additional successful test cases, either for this program or for future programs?

Again, this analysis process is difficult, but the answers discovered by it can be invaluable in improving subsequent programming efforts. It is alarming that the vast majority of programmers and programming organizations do not employ it.

REFERENCES

1. G. M. Weinberg, *The Psychology of Computer Programming*. New York: Van Nostrand Reinhold, 1971.
2. J. D. Gould and P. Drongowski, "A Controlled Psychological Study of Computer Program Debugging," RC-4083, IBM Research Division, Yorktown Heights, N.Y., 1972.
3. J. D. Gould, "Some Psychological Evidence on How People Debug Computer Programs," *Int. J. Man-Machine Stud.*, 7(2), 151–182 (1975).
4. A. R. Brown and W. A. Sampson, *Program Debugging*. London: Macdonald, 1973.

CHAPTER 8

Test Tools and Other Techniques

As discussed in prior chapters, the subject of test case design is considered to be the crux of software testing. Thus, most of the emphasis in the book is in this area. One remaining consideration is the degree to which the testing process can be automated. Unfortunately, the area of test case design has not yet been automated (e.g., no programs exist that accept a specification as input and produce a cause–effect graph or boundary-value analysis as output), but significant advances have been made in automating other aspects of the testing process.

This chapter summarizes and surveys automated testing and debugging tools, as well as other related techniques and ideas that were not covered in the earlier chapters. Its purpose is to give the student a perspective of what has been accomplished and where research activities are being directed, and to give the professional some guidance to the literature and away from attempts to "reinvent the wheel." Although the number of references in this chapter is large, in no way does it represent a *complete* survey; rather, sets of representative aids are discussed. If the reader wishes a more complete bibliography in a particular area, the bibliographies in one or two of the most recent references in that section should be examined.

MODULE DRIVER TOOLS

Module driver tools are an answer to a need discussed in Chapter 5: when testing a module or subroutine, one must write a small program to feed test-case inputs to the module. Rather than writing such programs, the module driver tool serves as a substitute by providing a language in which the test cases are expressed. Some driver tools also verify the results of each test case by allowing the user to specify the expected results of each test. The advantages of such tools are (1) the language reduces the effort required and standardizes the form of test cases, (2) test cases are easily rerun when a change or correction is made to the module, and (3) the automatic verification of results forces the programmer to state explicitly the expected output and lessens the "eye seeing what it wants to see" problem discussed in Chapter 2.

One sophisticated driver tool is AUT (Automated Unit Test) [1, 2, 8]. One uses AUT by encoding test cases (inputs and expected outputs) in a nonprocedural language and storing them in a data base. The module is tested by entering a single command from a terminal. This causes AUT to compile each test case, execute the module with the appropriate input, compare the actual output to the expected output, and report any discrepancies to the user.

AUT can also be used as a substitute for stubs in a top-down test. One does this by writing test cases for the nonexistent modules. When the program under test calls a nonexistent module, AUT traps the call, examines the inputs to the called module, tries to find a test case in the data base having the same inputs, and, providing one is found, sets up in storage the expected output described in the test case. Hence, AUT uses the test cases for the nonexistent module to simulate its action.

Other commercially available driver tools include MTS [3] and TESTMASTER. Other driver tools include a compiler for the SIMPL-T language in which one describes inputs and expected outputs in a "test" statement at the beginning of the module under test [4]; TPL/F and TPL/2.0, languages for writing Fortran driver modules and stubs [5, 6, 8]; and a driver tool for an assembly language [7].

REFERENCES

1. C. A. Heuermann, G. J. Myers, and J. H. Winterton, "Automated Test and Verification," *IBM Tech. Disclosure Bull.* 17(7), 2030–2035 (1974).
2. *Automated Unit Test (AUT) Program Description/Operation Manual.* SH20-1663. White Plains, N.Y.: IBM, 1975.
3. *Module Testing System (MTS) Fact Book.* London, England; Management Systems and Programming Limited, 1972.
4. R. G. Hamlet, "Testing Programs with the Aid of a Compiler," *IEEE Trans. Software Eng.,* SE-3(4), 279-290 (1977).
5. D. J. Panzl, "Test Procedures: A New Approach to Software Verification," *Proceedings of the Second International Conference on Software Engineering.* New York: IEEE, 1976, pp. 477–485.
6. *Fortran Test Procedure Language—Programmer Reference Manual.* Schenectady, N.Y.: General Electric, 1977.
7. D. Itoh and T. Izutani, "FADEBUG-I, A New Tool for Program Debugging," *Record of the 1973 IEEE Symposium on Computer Software Reliability.* New York: IEEE, 1973, pp. 38–43.
8. D. J. Panzl, "Automatic Software Test Drivers," *Computer,* 11(4), 44–50 (1978).

STATIC-FLOW-ANALYSIS TOOLS

Static flow analysis is a different and exciting type of test tool. It is performed by a program that investigates another program for errors, without executing the subject program. It can be likened to an automated code inspection. By analyzing a program's control and data flow, the analyzer can discover instances of such common problems as a reference to a variable having an undefined value, inconsistent interfaces among modules, variables that are assigned values that are never used, "unreachable" code (program statements that can never be executed), and violations of programming standards. For instance, the analysis of the Fortran subroutine

```
SUBROUTINE S(A,B)
VOLT=A+B
B=VOLTS
RETURN
END
```

by such a tool would result in a report of the reference to uninitialized variable VOLTS and the fact that VOLT is never referenced after being set.

The ASES tool [1, 2] reports unreachable code and instances of predefined error-prone programming practices (e.g., branching into a DO loop). RXVP [3] locates references to uninitialized variables in Fortran programs, inconsistencies between subroutine arguments and parameters, and denominators in arithmetic expressions that can potentially be 0. Another Fortran tool, AUDIT [4], detects references to uninitialized variables and violations of ANSI Fortran standards.

FACES [5, 6], another Fortran tool, checks each subroutine interface for consistent number and types of arguments and parameters, locates alignment errors in COMMON blocks, and identifies error-prone practices (e.g., passing a constant as an argument). In an initial application at NASA, FACES found approximately 1 error per 200 statements in a large Fortran program. In an analysis of software associated with NASA's space shuttle, FACES found problems in 6.5% of the statements [7]. DAVE [8–10], an additional Fortran tool, performs a similar analysis. Also, Wendel and Kleir [11] present a useful discussion of the objectives of static-flow-analysis tools.

REFERENCES

1. C. V. Ramamoorthy, R.E. Meeker, and J. Turner, "Design and Construction of an Automated Software Evaluation System," *Record of the 1973 IEEE Symposium on Computer Software Reliability.* New York: IEEE, 1973, pp. 28 –37.

2. R. E. Meeker and C.V. Ramamoorthy, "A Study in Software Reliability and Evaluation," Tech. Memo. No. 39, Electronics Research Center, University of Texas, 1973.

3. *RXVP User's Guide.* RM-1942, Santa Barbara, Cal.: General Research, 1975.

4. L. M. Culpepper, "A System for Reliable Engineering Software," *IEEE Trans. Software Eng.* SE-1(2), 174–178 (1975).

5. C. V. Ramamoorthy and S. F. Ho, "Fortran Automatic Code Evaluation System (FACES)," ERL-M466, University of California at Berkeley, 1974.

6. C. V. Ramamoorthy and S. F. Ho, "Testing Large Software with Automated Software Evaluation System," *IEEE Trans. Software Eng.,* SE-1(1), 46–58 (1975).

7. *NASA Software Specification and Evaluation System, Final Report.* Huntsville, Ala.: Science Applications, 1977 (NTIS N77-26828).

8. L. Osterweil and L.D. Fosdick, "Data Flow Analysis as an Aid in Documenting, Assertion, Generation, Validation, and Error Detection," CU-CS-055-74, University of Colorado, 1974.

9. L. J. Osterweil and L. D. Fosdick, "Some Experience with DAVE— A Fortran

Program Analyzer," *Proceedings of the 1976 National Computer Conference.* Montvale, N.J.: AFIPS Press, 1976, pp. 909–915.

10. L. D. Fosdick and L. J. Osterweil, "Data Flow Analysis in Software Reliability," *Comput. Surveys,* 8(3), 305–330 (1976).

11. I. K. Wendel and R. L. Kleir, "Fortran Error Detection through Static Analysis," *Software Eng. Notes,* 2(3), 22–28 (1977).

12. R.E. Fairly, "Tutorial: Static Analysis and Dynamic Testing of Computer Software," *Computer,* 11(4), 14–23 (1978).

TEST-COVERAGE MONITORS

Coverage monitors are aids that are applicable to white-box testing activities. They monitor the subject program during execution, providing statistics to determine if the statement-coverage and decision-coverage criteria have been met. (No known tools have been developed to monitor any of the condition-coverage criteria.) Most of the tools function by having a preprocessor insert probes (e.g., special subroutine calls) at particular points in the source program.

PET [1, 2], a Fortran monitor, produces a listing showing the number of times each statement was executed and the number of times each branch direction was taken. RXVP [3] does a similar thing for Fortran programs, as does FORTUNE, produced by the Capex Corporation. JAVS [4] performs a similar function for JOVIAL programs.

REFERENCES

1. L. G. Stucki, "Automatic Generation of Self-Metric Software," *Record of the 1973 IEEE Symposium on Computer Software Reliability.* New York: IEEE, 1973, pp. 94–100.

2. L. G. Stucki, "New Directions in Automated Tools for Improving Software Quality," *in* R. T. Yeh, ed., *Current Trends in Programming Methodology, Volume II, Program Validation.* Englewood Cliffs, N.J.: Prentice-Hall, 1977, pp. 80–111.

3. *RXVP User's Guide.* RM-1942. Santa Barbara, Cal.: General Research, 1975.

4. E. F. Miller, "Methodology for Comprehensive Software Testing," RADC-TR-75-161, General Research Corp., Santa Barbara, Cal., 1975 (NTIS AD/A-013111).

5. C. V. Ramamoorthy, K. H. Kim, and W. T. Chen, "Optimal Placement of Software Monitors Aiding Systematic Testing," *IEEE Trans. Software Eng.* SE-1(4), 403–411 (1975).

6. J. C. Huang, "Program Instrumentation and Software Testing," *Computer,* 11(4), 25–31 (1978).

MATHEMATICAL PROOFS OF PROGRAM CORRECTNESS

Given the fundamental problem of testing, that the best one can do is to find errors since it is impossible to show the absence of errors, the obvious wish is for an alternative to testing, for something that could actually demonstrate that a program is error free. This desire has resulted in the area of study known as *program proving* or *proofs of program correctness.*

The most common method of program proving is the *method of inductive assertions.* The goal is the development of a set of theorems about the program in question, the proof of which guarantees the absence of errors in the program. The method begins by requiring one to write *assertions* about the program's input conditions and correct results. The assertions are expressed symbolically in a formal logic system, usually the first-order predicate calculus. One then locates each loop in the program and, for each, writes an assertion stating the invariant (always true) conditions at an arbitrary point in the loop. The program has now been partitioned into a fixed number of fixed-length paths (all possible paths between a pair of assertions). For each path, one takes the assertion at either end of the path, moves it along the path using the semantics of the intervening program statements to modify the assertion, and eventually reaches the end of the path. At this point, two assertions exist at the end of the path: the original one and the one derived from the assertion at the opposite end. One then writes a theorem stating that the original assertion implies the derived assertion, and attempts to prove the theorem.

As mentioned above, the method of inductive assertions [1] is the most common proof technique. If the theorems can be proved, the statement is made that the program is error free (i.e., meets its input and output assertions) *providing that the program terminates.* A separate proof is necessary to show that the program will always eventually terminate [2]. Other proof techniques are the methods of *predicate transformers* [3, 4], *subgoal induction* [5], *computation induction* [6], *structural induction* [6, 7], and *intermittent assertions* [8]. London [9] provides a good overview and a list of 151 references.

Program proving is an exciting idea, one that may have profound influences on software development in the future, but it is not without problems. One problem is that it requires an enormous amount of intellectual effort. As a result, as of this time, no large programs have been proved correct, nor have proofs been applied to commercial production programs. The other problem is the validity of the claim of guaranteeing the absence of errors. This is still an open question and largely dependent on how one defines "error," but, to be objective, there are studies showing errors in published proofs [10], showing how proofs can be fallible [11], and showing why "proved" programs still need to be tested [12].

REFERENCES

1. R. W. Floyd, "Assigning Meaning to Programs," *Proceeding of the American Mathematical Society Symposium in Applied Mathematics, Volume 19.* Providence, R. I.: American Mathematical Society, 1967, pp. 19–31.

2. S. Katz and Z. Manna, "A Closer Look at Termination," *in* R. T. Yeh ed., *Current Trends in Programming Methodology, Volume II, Program Validation.* Englewood Cliffs, N.J.: Prentice-Hall, 1977, pp. 248–268.

3. S. K. Basu and R. T. Yeh, "Strong Verification of Programs," *IEEE Trans. Software Eng.*, SE-1(3), 339–346 (1975).

4. R. T. Yeh, "Verification of Programs by Predicate Transformation," *in* R. T. Yeh ed., *Current Trends in Programming Methodology, Volume II, Program Validation.* Englewood Cliffs, N.J.: Prentice-Hall, 1977, pp. 228–247.

5. J. H. Morris, Jr., and B. Wegbreit, "Program Verification by Subgoal Induction," *in* R. T. Yeh, ed., *Current Trends in Programming Methodology, Volume II, Program Validation.* Englewood Cliffs, N.J.: Prentice-Hall, 1977, pp. 197–227.

6. Z. Manna, S. Ness, and J. Vuillemin, "Inductive Methods for Proving Properties of Programs," *Commun. ACM,* 16(8), 491–502 (1973).

7. C. Reynolds and R. T. Yeh, "Induction as the Basis for Program Verification," *IEEE Trans. Software Eng.* SE-2(4), 244–252 (1976).

8. Z. Manna and R. Waldinger, "Is 'Sometime' Sometimes Better than 'Always'?" *Commun. ACM,* 21(2), 159–172 (1978).

9. R. L. London, "Perspective on Program Verification," *in* R. T. Yeh ed., *Current Trends in Programming Methodology, Volume II, Program Validation.* Englewood Cliffs, N.J.: Prentice-Hall, 1977, pp. 151–172.

10. S. L. Gerhart and L. Yelowitz, "Observations of Fallibility in Applications of Modern Programming Methodologies," *IEEE Trans. Software Eng.* SE-2(3), 195–207 (1976).

11. J. B. Goodenough and S. L. Gerhart, "Toward a Theory of Test Data Selection," *IEEE Trans. Software Eng.* SE-1(2), 156–173 (1975).

12. A. S. Tanenbaum, "In Defense of Program Testing, or Correctness Proofs Considered Harmful," *SIGPLAN Not.,* 11(5), 64–68 (1976).

13. L. Robinson and K. N. Levitt, "Proof Techniques for Hierarchically Structured Programs," *in* R. T. Yeh, ed., *Current Trends in Programming Methodology, Volume II, Program Validation.* Englewood Cliffs, N.J.: Prentice-Hall, 1977, pp. 173–196.

14. C. A. R. Hoare, "Proof of a Program: FIND," *Commun. ACM,* 14(1), 39-45 (1971).

15. L. Lampert, "Proving the Correctness of Multiprocess Programs," *IEEE Trans. Software Eng.*, SE-3(2), 125–143 (1977).

16. B. Wegbreit, "Constructive Methods in Program Verification," *IEEE Trans. Software Eng.* SE-3(3), 193–209 (1977).

17. D. Gries, "An Illustration of Current Ideas on the Derivation of Correctness Proofs and Correct Programs," *IEEE Trans. Software Eng.* SE-2(4), 238–244 (1976).

18. C. D. Allen, "The Application of Formal Logic to Programs and Programming," *IBM Systems J.* 10(1), 2–38 (1971).

19. B. Elspas, K. N. Levitt, R. J. Waldinger, and A. Waksman, "An Assessment of Techniques for Proving Program Correctness," *Comput. Surveys,* 4(2), 97–147 (1972).

PROGRAM CORRECTNESS PROVERS

Since the process of program proving involves a lot of formula manipulations and seemingly tedious clerical work, an obvious extension is the automation of much of this process. The original goal was to devise a program that, given another program and its input and output assertions, would attempt to prove the subject program correct. Hence the correctness provers would have to devise the inductive assertions, generate the necessary theorems by manipulating assertions over the semantics of the subject program, and prove the theorems.

Current efforts have backed away from this goal, largely because producing the inductive assertions and proving the theorems requires considerable (humanlike) intelligence. Hence, current program provers are interactive tools, proceeding until they hit a stumbling block and then asking the human user for assistance.

The pioneering effort in this area is a fully automated theorem generator and prover for programs written in a subset of the Algol language [1]. The proof system developed by Good, London, and Bledsoe [2] is more representative of current lines of thought. Its theorem prover contains a time limit. If it cannot prove a theorem in this time, the user is asked to examine the incomplete proof and supply the system with suggestions as to how to proceed.

REFERENCES

1. J. C. King, "A Program Verifier," Ph.D. dissertation, Carnegie-Mellon University, 1969.

2. D. I. Good, R. L. London, and W. W. Bledsoe, "An Interactive Program Verification System," *IEEE Trans. Software Eng.* SE-1(1), 59–67 (1975).

3. J. C. King, "Proving Programs to be Correct," *IEEE Trans. Comput.* C-20(11), 1331–1336 (1971).

4. L. P. Deutsch, "An Interactive Program Verifier," Ph.D. dissertation, University of California at Berkeley, 1973.

5. B. Elspas, K. N. Levitt, and R. J. Waldinger, "An Interactive System for the Verification of Computer Programs," Final report, Project 1891, Stanford Research Institute, Stanford, Cal., 1973.

6. R. S. Boyer and J. S. Moore, "Proving Theorems about LISP Functions," *J. ACM,* 22(1), 129–144 (1975).

7. S. M. German and B. Wegbreit, "A Synthesizer of Inductive Assertions," *IEEE Trans. Software Eng.* SE-1(1), 68–75 (1975).

SYMBOLIC EXECUTION

Symbolic execution is a hybrid, a cross between program testing and correctness provers. The subject program is executed, but it is executed symbolically. That is, variables can take on symbolic, as well as numeric, values. A symbolic value is an algebraic idetifier or an expression containing symbolic and numeric values. For instance, when executing the following program segment

```
SUBROUTINE COMP(PRICE,RAGE,VAL)
SURC=.1
PRICE=PRICE*SURC/VAL
RANGE=PRICE*VAL*20 + 2
END
```

the input variables PRICE and VAL can be assigned the algebraic values A and B. After execution completes, the symbolic values of PRICE, RANGE, and VAL are $.01A/B$, $.2A + 2$, and B, respectively. In other words, the test case inputs can be expressed symbolically, and the expected output is expressed as a symbolic relationship of the input values.

The obvious problem is how the tool handles branching statements, such as IF statements, where the path taken is dependent on *specific* values of the variables. To illustrate the solution, if the statement

IF (PRICE>0) ...

is encountered, the normal approach is the following. If the system knows that PRICE>0, or if it can deduce whether PRICE>0, it takes the appropriate path. If not, it asks the user for guidance. If the user instructs the system to take the *true* path, the system adds the condition PRICE>0 to the symbolic state of the program and resumes executing at the THEN path.

The EFFIGY system [1, 2] symbolically executes programs written in a subset of PL/I; SELECT [3] does the same for programs written in a subset of LISP; and DISSECT [4–7] does the same for FORTRAN programs. Another symbolic executer [8] is part of the DAVE system referenced in the section on static flow analysis.

REFERENCES

1. J. C. King, "A New Approach to Program Testing," *Proceedings of the 1975 International Conference on Reliable Software.* New York: IEEE, 1975, pp. 228–233.

2. J. C. King, "Symbolic Execution and Program Testing," *Commun. ACM,* 19(7), 385–394 (1976).

3. R. S. Boyer, B. Elspas, and K. N. Levitt, "SELECT—A Formal System for Testing and Debugging Programs by Symbolic Execution," *Proceedings of the 1975 International Conference on Reliable Software.* New York: IEEE, 1975, pp. 234–245.

4. W. E. Howden, "Methodology for the Generation of Program Test Data," *IEEE Trans. Comput.,* C-24(5), 554–560 (1975).

5. W. E. Howden, "Experiments with a Symbolic Evaluation System," *Proceedings of the 1976 National Computer Confrence.* Montvale, N.J.: AFIPS Press, 1976, pp. 899–908.

6. W. E. Howden, "Symbolic Testing and the DISSECT Symbolic Evaluation System," *IEEE Trans. Software Eng.* SE-3(4), 266–278 (1977).

7. W. E. Howden, "DISSECT—A Symbolic Evaluation and Program Testing System," *IEEE Trans. Software Eng.* SE-4(1), 70–73 (1978).

8. L. A. Clarke, "A System to Generate Test Data and Symbolically Execute Programs," *IEEE Trans. Software Eng.,* SE-2(3), 215–222 (1976).

9. S. L. Hantler and J.C. King, "An Introduction to Proving the Correctness of Programs," *Comput. Surveys,* 8(3), 331–353 (1976).

10. C. V. Ramamoorthy, S. F. Ho, and W. T. Chen, "On the Automated Generation of Program Test Data," *IEEE Trans. Software Eng.* SE-2(4), 293–300 (1976).

11. J. A. Darringer and J. C. King, "Applications of Symbolic Execution to Program Testing," *Computer,* 11(4), 51–60 (1978).

TEST DATA GENERATORS

As mentioned earlier, there are no known tools that can automatically design test cases by performing equivalence partitioning, cause–effect graphing, or boundary-value analysis on a specification. For a lack of anything else, one could envision a tool that generates random streams of input data for a subject program. Such programs exist, but they are not mentioned here because they represent, at best, an inefficient and ad hoc approach to testing.

However, numerous tools have been developed to assist the designer in identifying and/or formulating test data. Note that care has been taken to label such tools as test *data* generators, not test *case* generators, since even the most sophisticated of them do not actually generate test cases (i.e., inputs and expected outputs).

One set of test data generators is white-box oriented, that is, they analyze a program's logic flow and deduce, for instance, the sets of input data needed to achieve a specified criterion. Previous efforts include proposed tools that, given certain criteria such as "execute this path" or "achieve the decision-coverage criterion," deduce the necessary input values [1, 2] and a general discussion of the implementation of such a tool [3]. Another tool does not generate test data, but it identifies, for a subject Fortran subroutine, the minimum number of paths that must be executed to achieve decision coverage [4].

Other test data generators aid the tester in producing test cases. One contains an Englishlike language that is used to describe the desired contents of a file [5]. The language is then processed, yielding a PL/I program that creates the file. Another generates test data for a compiler, given a description of its input (programming language) in a formal grammar [6]. A third tool deduces, from a description of a program in a specification language, a set of nonredundant test inputs [7].

REFERENCES

1. H. N. Gabow, S. N. Maheshwari, and L. J. Osterweil, "On Two Problems in the Generation of Program Test Paths," *IEEE Trans. Software Eng.* SE-2(3), 227–231 (1976).

2. J. C. Huang, "An Approach to Program Testing," *Comput. Surveys,* 7(3), 113–128 (1975).

3. C. V. Ramamoorthy, S. F. Ho, and W. T. Chen, "On the Automated Generation of Program Test Data," *IEEE Trans. Software Eng.* SE-2(3), 215–222 (1976).

4. K. W. Krause, R. W. Smith, and M. A. Goodwin, "Optimal Software Test Planning Through Automated Network Analysis," *Record of the 1973 IEEE Symposium on Computer Software Reliability.* New York: IEEE, 1973, pp. 18–22.

5. N. R. Lyons, "An Automatic Data Generation System for Data Base Simulation and Testing," *Data Base,* 8(4), 10–13 (1977).

6. B. Houssais, "Verification of an Algol 68 Implementation," *Proceedings of the Strathclyde Algol 68 Conference.* New York: ACM, 1977, pp. 117–128.

7. R. J. Peterson, "TESTER/1: An Abstract Model for the Automatic Synthesis of Program Test Case Specifications," *Proceedings of the Symposium on Computer Software Engineering.* New York: Polytechnic Press, 1976, pp. 465–484.

8. W. H. Jessop, J. R. Kane, S. Roy, and J. M. Scanlon, "ATLAS—An Automated Software Testing System," *Proceedings of the Second International Conference on Software Engineering.* New York: IEEE, 1976, pp. 629–635.

9. W. Miller and D. L. Spooner, "Automatic Generation of Floating-Point Test Data," *IEEE Trans. Software Eng.* SE-2(3), 223–226 (1976).

ENVIRONMENTAL SIMULATORS

An environmental simulator is a tool that simulates the environment surrounding a system when testing in a live environment is impractical or too costly. It is used primarily in the system-test phase for (1) stress and volume tests (e.g., to simulate the actions of 100 terminal users on a timesharing system), (2) creating test conditions that are difficult or impossible to create in a real environment (e.g., specific hardware failures), and (3) when testing in a live environment is out of the question (e.g., testing nuclear-reactor control programs, aerospace systems, air defense systems).

Many computer manufacturers use and/or sell terminal simulators: programs that reside in a separate, connected computer and simulate the actions of terminal users. As examples of a few specialized simulators, one was developed for the testing of the New York City Fire Department's dispatching system [1], a system that processes fire alarms, dispatches equipment, and adjusts fire-fighting coverage; another was used to simulate attacks during the testing of an air-defense system [2]; a third was used to test the flight computer in the United States NASA space shuttle [3]; and a fourth simulator was used to test the flight computer software in the Saturn rocket [4]. PRIM [5] is a simulator of a nonexistent central processing unit; it is a general-purpose emulator on which one can define and microprogram a target computer architecture.

REFERENCES

1. J. Mohan and M. Geller, "An Environmental Simulator for the FDNY Computer-Aided Dispatch System," *Proceedings of the Second International Conferences on Software Engineering.* New York: IEEE, 1976, pp. 577–584.

2. R. T. Stevens, "Testing the NORAD Command and Control System," *IEEE Trans. Systems Sci. Cyber.* SSC-4(1), 47–51 (1968).

3. L. W. Drane, B. J. McCoy, and L. W. Silver, "Design of the Software Development and Verification System (SWDVS) for Shuttle NASA Study Task 35-S," R-721, Draper Laboratory, Cambridge, Mass., 1972 (NTIS N75-12038).

4. J. H. Jacobs and T. J. Dillon, "Interactive Saturn Flight Program Simulator," *IBM Systems J.* 9(2), 145–158 (1970).

5. L. Gallenson et al.,"PRIM User's Manual," ISI/TM-75-1, Information Sciences Institute, University of Southern California, 1975 (NTIS AD/A-009936).

SNEAK-CIRCUIT ANALYSIS

The possibility of analogs between software development and electrical engineering is an old idea, and leads one to search for engineering methodologies and tools that might be applied to programming. One such engineering tool is *sneak-circuit analysis,* a process that locates flaws in electronic-circuit designs. By developing electrical analogies of software structures (e.g., a branch is a switch, a data reference is a relay contact, an assignment is a resistor), a tool was developed to find sneak circuits in software [1]. The types of errors detected by the tool include references to undefined values and the use of data as addresses.

REFERENCES

1. J. P. Rankin, G. J. Engles, and S. G. Godoy, "Software Sneak Circuit Analysis," AFNL-TR-75-254, Boeing Aerospace Co., Houston Texas, 1976 (NTIS AD/A-024718).

VIRTUAL MACHINES

Virtual machines, a type of environmental simulator, are implemented by a hypervisor program that gives multiple programs the impression that each is executing in a separate, stand-alone machine. Hence, they allow the simultaneous testing of multiple operating systems on one physical machine, or the testing of a new operating system in the same physical machine that is concurrently running production programs. In addition to this advantage of parallelism (i.e., the illusion of multiple real machines), they allow one to use an interactive terminal as an operator's console, to test from the office instead of the computing center and in the day rather than the wee hours of the night, and the hypervisor usually provides debugging tools not present in a barren real machine.

REFERENCES

1. J. P. Buzen and U. O. Gagliardi, "The Evolution of Virtual Machine Architecture," *Proceedings of the 1973 National Computer Conference*. Montvale, N.J.: AFIPS Press, 1973, pp. 291–299.
2. S. W. Galley and R.P. Goldberg, "Software Debugging: The Virtual Machine Approach," *Proceedings of the ACM 1974 Annual Conference*. New York: ACM, 1974, pp. 395–400.
3. J. D. Bagley, "The SPY—An Extended Virtual Machine," RC-5310, IBM Research Div., Yorktown Heights, N.Y., 1975.

TESTING MATHEMATICAL SOFTWARE

The testing of mathematical software presents one with some unique problems. Here, because of the finite precision of computer arithmetic, the inexact representation of numbers in a binary computer, and the use of finite computations to represent infinite mathematical processes, one cannot always predict the precise expected output of each test case. Hence, such tests are concerned with measuring accuracy, roundoff errors, and the correlation of errors. The references below survey these problems.

REFERENCES

1. W. J. Cody, "The Evaluation of Mathematical Software," *in* W. C. Hetzel, ed., *Program Test Methods*. Englewood Cliffs, N.J.: Prentice-Hall, 1973, pp. 121–133.
2. E. W. Ng, "Mathematical Software Testing Activities," *in* W. C. Hetzel, ed., *Program Test Methods*. Englewood Cliffs, N.J.: Prentice-Hall, 1973, pp. 135–141.
3. H. S. Bright and I. J. Cole, "A Method of Testing Programs for Data Sensitivity," *in* W. C. Hetzel, ed., *Program Test Methods*. Englewood Cliffs, N.J.: Prentice-Hall, 1973, pp. 143–162.
4. W. L. Sadowski and D. W. Lozier, "A Unified Standards Approach to Algorithm Testing," *in* W. C. Hetzel, ed., *Program Test Methods*. Englewood Cliffs, N.J.: Prentice-Hall, 1973, pp. 277–290.
5. T. J. Hull, W. H. Enright, and A. E. Sedgwick, "The Correctness of Numerical Algorithms," *SIGPLAN Not.* 7(1), 66–73 (1972).
6. W. Miller and D. L. Spooner, "Automatic Generation of Floating-Point Test Data," *IEEE Trans. Software Eng.* SE-2(3), 223–226 (1976).

7. M. A. Hennell, D. Hedley, and M. R. Woodward, "Experience with an Algol 68 Numerical Algorithms Testbed," *Proceedings of the Symposium on Computer Software Engineering.* New York: Polytechnic Press, 1976, pp. 457–463.

SOFTWARE ERROR STUDIES

As was pointed out in Chapter 7, studies of software errors can be invaluable in improving future design and testing processes. Also, as mentioned in Chapter 6, error data from previous projects are useful in answering one of the most difficult questions: When do I stop testing? Unfortunately, such data are rather scarce; the majority of the studies mentioned below come from government projects where the analysis of errors was necessary to satisfy the contract for the software system.

Large-scale studies include a classification of 2165 errors in a large radar control system [1], 1189 errors in a university experiment involving the development of small programs written in Fortran, PL/I, Algol, Basic, and Cobol [2], a study of errors in three large software packages [3], and a study of errors in four large programs produced by TRW Systems [4]. Another interesting study analyzes the errors found during the testing of a release of IBM's DOS/VS operating system [5]. In addition to classifying the errors, the probable causes of the errors were studied, and predictions were made of the most effective methods to prevent or detect the errors earlier.

An early language study involved the coding of two versions of seven programs [6]. One version was coded in PL/I; the other was coded in Fortran, Cobol, or Jovial. The study report discusses each of the errors found during the experiment; the errors are summarized in reference 7. Another language study, a study of the relationships between errors and language-design tradeoffs, also discusses the errors encountered [8]. Another effort [7], although not primarily an error study, discusses 27 types of semantic errors that are not detected by most compilers and contains an "expert consensus estimate" of the relative frequencies of semantic, specification, and logical errors and the distribution, across the lifetime of the program, of when the three classes of errors are usually detected. It also summarizes other error studies and contains a study of 38 errors in a PL/I application program.

Other studies include data from an unspecified set of projects [9], a sample of 39 errors from avionics systems and a marinetraffic control system [10], 5 common list-processing errors [11], errors found when testing a small operating system [12], syntax errors [13, 14], semantic errors in PL/C programs [15], and errors in an assembly-language control program [16]. A study of 2036 errors in a 120,000-statement avionics control program [17] showed that 50% of the errors were design mistakes and 6% were due to corrections of prior problems. It also showed that 85% of the corrections involved the alteration of only a single module (a result confirmed in reference 5).

REFERENCES

1. H. E. Willman, Jr., et al., "Software Systems Reliability: A Raytheon Project History," RADC-TR-77-188, Raytheon Corp., Bedford, Mass., 1977 (NTIS AD/A-040992).

2. E. A. Youngs, "Human Errors in Programming," *Int. J. Man-Machine Stud.* 6(3), 361–376 (1974).

3. G. R. Craig et al., "Software Reliability Study," RADC-TR-74-250, TRW Systems Group, Redondo Beach, Cal., 1974 (NTIS AD/A-787784).

4. T. A. Thayer et al., "Software Reliability Study," RADC-TR-76-238, TRW Defense and Space Systems Group, Redondo Beach, Cal., 1976 (NTIS AD/A-030798).

5. A. Endres, "An Analysis of Errors and Their Causes in System Programs," *IEEE Trans. Software Eng.*, SE-1(2), 140–149 (1975).

6. R. J. Rubey et al., "Comparative Evaluation of PL/I," ESD-TR-68-150, U.S. Air Force, Bedford, Mass., 1968.

7. G. J. Myers, "The Design of Computer Architectures to Enhance Software Reliability," Ph.D. dissertation, Polytechnic Institute of New York, 1977.

8. J. D. Gannon and J. J. Horning, "Language Design for Programming Reliability," *IEEE Trans. Software Eng.*, SE-1(2), 179–191 (1975).

9. R. J. Rubey, J. A. Dana, and P. W. Biche, "Quantitative Aspects of Software Validation," *IEEE Trans. Software Eng.*, SE-1(2), 150–155 (1975).

10. J. P. Rankin, G. J. Engels, and S. G. Godoy, "Software Sneak Circuit Analysis," AFWL-75-254, Boeing Aerospace Co., Houston, Texas, 1976.

11. J. Palme, "List Structures in SIMULA and PL/I—A Comparison," *Software Prac. Exper.*, 4(4), 379–388 (1974).

12. D. Itoh and T. Izutani, "FADEBUG-I, A New Tool for Program Debugging," *Record of the 1973 IEEE Symposium on Computer Software Reliability.* New York: IEEE, 1973, pp. 38–43.

13. S. J. Boies and J. D. Gould, "A Behavioral Analysis of Programming—On the Frequency of Syntactical Errors," RC-3907, IBM Research Div., Yorktown Heights, N.Y., 1972.

14. C. R. Litecky and G. B. Davis, "A Study of Errors, Error-Proneness, and Error Diagnosis in Cobol," *Commun. ACM*, 19(1), 33–37 (1976).

15. G. Estrin, R. R. Muntz, and R. C. Uzgalis, "Modeling, Measurement, and Computer Power," *Proceedings of the 1972 Spring Joint Computer Conference*, Montvale, N.J.: AFIPS Press. 1972, pp. 725–738.

16. M. I. Shooman and M. I. Bolsky, "Types, Distribution, and Test and Correction Times for Programming Errors," *Proceedings of the 1975 International Conference on Reliable Software.* New York: IEEE, 1975, pp. 347–357.

17. M. J. Fries, "Software Error Data Acquisition," RADC-TR-77-130, Boeing Aerospace Co., Seattle, Wash., 1977 (NTIS AD/A-039916).

SOFTWARE-ERROR DATA COLLECTION

As discussed in Chapter 7, it is imperative that programming organizations collect and analyze data about their own errors. In doing so, methods for the classification of errors are important. Some of the error studies [1–3] discuss their classification schemes. There exist proposals for methods of studying and classifying errors [4], as well as discussions of the problems in developing classification schemes [5]. Curry [6] discusses a method used to measure the effectiveness of development and testing tools in finding particular types of errors. An eight-volume proposal to establish a repository of software data [7] is broader in scope (i.e., collecting data on costs and productivity), but it does include a discussion of error collection. Finally, Chapter 7 of this book discusses a procedure for analyzing errors.

REFERENCES

1. T. A. Thayer et al., "Software Reliability Study," RADC-TR-76-238, TRW Defense and Space Systems Group, Redondo Beach, Cal., 1976 (NTIS AD/A-030798).

2. G. R. Craig et al., "Software Reliability Study," RADC-TR-74-250, TRW Systems Group, Redondo Beach, Cal., 1974, (NTIS AD/A-787784).

3. R. J. Rubey, J. A. Dana, and P. W. Biche, "Quantitative Aspects of Software Validation," *IEEE Trans. Software Eng.* SE-1(2), 150–155 (1975).

4. W. Amory and J. A. Clapp, "Engineering of Quality Software Systems, Volume VII, A Software Error Classification Methodology," RADC-TR-74-325, Mitre Corp., Bedford, Mass., 1975 (NTIS AD/A-007772).

5. S. L. Gerhart, "Development of a Methodology for Classifying Software Errors," Duke University, Durham, N.C., 1976 (NTIS N76-26896).

6. R. W. Curry, "A Measure to Support Calibration and Balancing of the Effectiveness of Software Engineering Tools and Techniques," *Proceedings of the Symposium on Computer Software Engineering.* New York: Polytechnic, 1976, pp. 199–214.

7. N. E. Willmorth, M. C. Finfer, and M. P. Templeton, "Software Data Collection Study, Summary and Conclusions," RADC-TR-76-329, System Development Corp., Santa Monica, Cal., 1976 (NTIS AD/A-036115).

PREDICTIVE MODELS

Of all the unknowns facing a project manager, perhaps the most significant one is knowledge of the number of errors remaining in a program. Not only would a reasonable estimate of this help one in determining when to stop testing, but it could be used to estimate the maintenance costs after the program is placed into production, and estimate the program's reliability and mean time to failure.

Existing predictive models fall into three general categories: (1) models that are derived from hardware-reliability models, (2) models that are based on the structure of the program, and (3) "error-seeding" models. The basic model [1, 2] in the first category comes directly from hardware-reliability theory. Further refinements have been added to this model [3, 4], its use as a determination of when to stop testing has been proposed [5], and it has been tested on a code-reading experiment [6].

Other reliability models have been based on Markov processes [7, 8]. One study [9] compares actual error data from a large command and control system to predictions from several models. A small set of models falls in the second category, models that are derived from the internal structure of the program. As an example, one [10] employs multiple linear-regression analysis to predict the number of errors. The parameters in the model include the program's size, number of branch statements, levels of nesting, and number of data types referenced.

A totally different type of predictive model is based on statistical sampling theory. Such models are known as *error-seeding models.* By purposely seeding (injecting) errors into a program and then counting the number of seeded versus original errors detected, one can estimate the total number of original errors. This model is also known as the "fishpond model," since it is identical to the sampling problem often seen in statistics textbooks of estimating the number of yellow perch in a pond. The original model is discussed by Mills [11]; subsequent refinements have been made [12–15]. One discussion [15] shows how to use the model by having two independent groups test the program, rather than seeding errors into the program.

REFERENCES

1. Z. Jelinski and P. B. Moranda, "Software Reliability Research," *in* W. Freiberger, ed., *Statistical Computer Performance Evaluation.* New York: Academic, 1972, pp. 465–484.

2. M. L. Shooman, "Operational Testing and Software Reliability Estimation During Program Development," *Record of the 1973 IEEE Symposium on Computer Software Reliability.* New York: IEEE, 1973, pp. 51–57.

3. M. L. Shooman and S. Natarajan, "Effect of Manpower Deployment and Bug Generation on Software Error Models," *Proceedings of the Symposium on Computer Software Engineering.* New York: Polytechnic, 1976, pp. 155–170.

4. M. L. Shooman, 'Structural Models for Software Reliability Prediction," *Proceedings of the Second International Conference on Software Engineering.* New York: IEEE, 1976, pp. 268–280.

5. E. H. Forman and N. D. Singpurwalla, "An Empirical Stopping Rule for Debugging and Testing Computer Software," T-320, The George Washington University, 1975 (NTIS AD/A-016027).

6. Z. Jelinski and P. B. Moranda, "Applications of a Probability-Based Model to a Code Reading Experiment," *Record of the 1973 IEEE Symposium on Computer Software Reliability.* New York: IEEE, 1973, pp. 78–81.

7. B. Littlewood, "A Semi-Markov Model for Software Reliability with Failure Costs," *Proceedings of the Symposium on Computer Software Engineering.* New York: Polytechnic Press, 1976, pp. 281–300.

8. A. K. Trivedi and M. L. Shooman, "A Markov Model for the Evaluation of Computer Software Performance," PI-EE/EP-74-011-EER110, Polytechnic Institute of New York, 1974.

9. A. N. Sukert, "A Software Reliability Modeling Study," RADC-TR-76-247, Rome Air Development Center, Griffiss Air Force Base, N.Y., 1976 (NTIS AD/A-030437).

10. R. W. Motley and W. D. Brooks, "Statistical Prediction of Programming Errors," RADC-TR-77-175, IBM Corp., Arlington, Va., 1977 (NTIS AD/A-041106).

11. H. D. Mills, "On the Statistical Validation of Computer Programs," FSC-72-6015, IBM Federal Systems Div., Gaithersburg, Md., 1972.

12. F. R. Richards, "Computer Software: Testing, Reliability Models, and Quality Assurance," NPS55RH74071A, Naval Postgraduate School, Monterey, Cal., 1974 (NTIS AD/A-001260).

13. B. Rudner, "Seeding/Tagging Estimation of Software Errors: Models and Estimates," RADC-TR-77-15, Polytechnic Institute of New York, 1977 (NTIS AD/A-036655).

14. L. J. LaPadula, "Engineering of Quality Software Systems, Volume VIII, Software Reliability Modeling and Measurement Techniques," RADC-TR-74-325, Mitre Corp., Bedford, Mass., 1975 (NTIS AD/A-007773).

15. G. J. Myers, *Software Reliability: Principles and Practices.* New York: Wiley–Interscience, 1976, Chapter 18.

16. N. F. Schneidewind, "Analysis of Error Processes in Computer Software," *Proceedings of the 1975 International Conference on Reliable Software.* New York: IEEE, 1975, pp. 337–346.

17. J. D. Musa, "A Theory of Software Reliability and its Application," *IEEE Trans. Software Eng.,* SE-1(3), 312–327 (1975).

18. B. Littlewood, "How to Measure Software Reliability, and How Not To," *Proceedings of the Third International Conference on Software Engineering.* New York: IEEE, 1978, pp. 37–45.

COMPLEXITY MEASURES

In addition to estimating the number of errors in the program, it would be useful to be able to quantify the complexity of the program or individual modules within the program (e.g., to predict the error-prone sections).

Most complexity measures (e.g., reference 1) are derived from the program's control flow (e.g., number of paths). One measure of this type, the *cyclomatic number,* provides one with an easy-to-compute estimate of control-flow complexity [2, 3, 10]. Other measures use regression analysis [4, 5], where the parameters reflect the structural aspects of the program, such as the number of data types, branches, and levels of nesting. One regression model [5] uses as parameters the extent to which the object code and source code could be reduced by restructuring the source code.

A microscopic theory of software structure called "software physics" counts the total number of operators and operands in a program and the number of unique operators and operands, and from these derives such measures as the "volume" of the program [6]. Other measures deal with the program on a more macroscopic level, that is, by analyzing its module, rather than logic, structure [7-9].

REFERENCES

1. J. E. Sullivan, "Measuring the Complexity of Computer Software," MTR-2648, Mitre Corp., Bedford, Mass., 1973.
2. T. J. McCabe, "A Complexity Measure," *IEEE Trans. Software Eng.,* SE-2(4), 308–320 (1976).
3. G. J. Myers, "An Extension to the Cyclomatic Measure of Program Complexity," *SIGPLAN Not.,* 12(10), 61–64 (1977).
4. R. W. Motley and W. D. Brooks, "Statistical Prediction of Programming Errors," RADC-TR-77-175, IBM Corp., Arlington, Va., 1977 (NTIS AD/A-041106).
5. S. J. Amster, E. J. Davis, B. N. Dickman, and J. P. Kuoni, "An Experiment in Automatic Quality Evaluation of Software," *Proceedings of the Symposium on Computer Software Engineering.* New York: Polytechnic, 1976, pp. 171–197.
6. M. H. Halstead, *Elements of Software Science.* New York: Elsevier, 1977.
7. A. E. Ferdinand, "A Theory of System Complexity," *Int. J. Gen. Systems,* 1(1), 19–33 (1974).
8. F. M. Haney, "Module Connection Analysis—A Tool for Scheduling Software Debugging Activities," *Proceedings of the 1972 Fall Joint Computer Conference.* Montvale, N.J.: AFIPS Press, 1972 pp. 173–179.

9. G. J. Myers, *Reliable Software through Composite Design.* New York: Petro-celli/Charter, 1975, Chapter 10.

10. W. J. Hansen, "Measurement of Program Complexity by the Pair (Cyclomatic Number, Operator Count)," *SIGPLAN Not,* 13(3), 29-33 (1978).

11. C. L. McClure, "A Model for Program Complexity," *Proceedings of the Third International Conference on Software Engineering.* New York: IEEE, 1978, pp. 149-157.

PROGRAM LIBRARY SYSTEMS

A program library system is an automated way of managing the code, documentation, and test cases produced during the development of a program. It normally consists of a data base and a set of auxiliary programs, such as editors, compilers, text formatters, and management tools. Although it is applicable to a broader range of activities than just the testing processes, it is mentioned here because it can be used as a library to maintain test cases, and because it is an indispensible tool in any large programming project.

The most widely used library systems appear to be PANVA-LET, produced by Pansophic Systems, and LIBRARIAN, produced by Applied Data Research. The Software Factory [1] is probably the most advanced library system produced to date. Other library systems include PDS [2] and SCCS [3, 4]; proposals exist for other library systems [5, 6]. A related system is Simon [7]; although not a library system, it is a set of data collection and reporting functions that one would hope to see in a powerful library system.

REFERENCES

1. H. Bratman, "The Software Factory," *Computer,* 8(5), 28-37 (1975).

2. C. G. Davis and C. R. Vick, "The Software Development System," *IEEE Trans. Software Eng.,* SE-3(1), 69-84 (1977).

3. M. J. Rochkind, "The Source Code Control System," *IEEE Trans. Software Eng.,* SE-1(4), 364-370 (1975).

4. T. A. Dolotta and J. R. Mashey, "An Introduction to the Programmer's Workbench," *Proceedings of the Second International Conference on Software Engineering.* New York: IEEE, 1976, pp. 164-168.

5. L. W. Drane, B. J. McCoy, and L. W. Silver, "Design of the Software Development and Verification System (SWDVS) for Shuttle NASA Study Task 35-S," R-721, Draper Laboratory, Cambridge, Mass., 1972 (NTIS N75-12038).

6. N. Tinanoff and F. M. Luppino, "Structured Programming Series, Volume VI, Programming Support Library (PSL) Program Specifications," RADC-

TR-74-300, IBM Federal Systems Div., Gaithersburg, Md., 1974 (NTIS AD/A-007796).

7. R. J. Fleischer and R. W. Spitler, "SIMON: A Project Management System for Software Development," *Proceedings of the Symposium on Computer Software Engineering.* New York: Polytechnic, 1976, pp. 547–560.

TESTING EXPERIMENTS

Given the large amount of money expended testing programs (literally billions of dollars per year), one would expect that many controlled experiments would have been performed to identify the most effective tools, methodologies, types of personnel, and so on. However, quite the opposite is the case; only a handful of experiments have appeared in the literature.

One experiment employed 39 subjects testing three programs [1]. Three methods were employed: black-box testing, white-box testing, and individual code reading. The major result was that the first two appeared equal in effectiveness and code reading was found to be inferior. On the average, the subjects found about half of the errors in the programs.

Another experiment employed 59 highly experienced subjects testing one program [2]. Three methods were used: black-box testing, a combination of black- and white-box testing, and three-person code inspections. In terms of errors found, the three methods were found to be equal in effectiveness, but the inspection method was less effective in terms of time expended. The experiment was extended to analyze independent two-party tests, where two people would independently test the program using the same or different methods and then their errors found and time expended are pooled. The independent two-party tests were found to be more effective than the basic methods in terms of errors found, and as effective in terms of labor time per error found. (The reason they did not increase the labor time per error was the high variability among subjects in terms of the particular errors found.) In terms of the number of errors found, the experiment showed a surprisingly large variability among the highly experienced subjects. Also, on the average, a little more than a third of the errors in the program were found.

Another experiment [3] contradicts a principle in Chapter 2 in that it shows that the testing of a program by a second party is neither more nor less effective than the testing by the original programmer. However, since only three subjects were used, the results are questionable. Another experiment found that the use of a module driver tool reduced working time by 11% during the module-test phase [4].

REFERENCES

1. W. C. Hetzel, "An Experimental Analysis of Program Verification Methods," Ph.D. dissertation, University of North Carolina at Chapel Hill, 1976.
2. G. J. Myers, "A Controlled Experiment in Program Testing and Code Walk-throughs/Inspections," *Commun. ACM*, 21(9), 760–768 (1978).
3. J. D. Musa, "An Exploratory Experiment with 'Foreign' Debugging of Programs," *Proceedings of the Symposium on Computer Software Engineering.* New York: Polytechnic, 1976, pp. 499–511.
4. D. Itoh and T. Izutani, "FADEBUG-I, A New Tool for Program Debugging," *Record of the 1973 IEEE Symposium on Computer Software Reliability.* New York: IEEE, 1973, pp. 38–43.
5. Z. Jelinski and P. B. Moranda, "Applications of a Probability-Based Model to a Code Reading Experiment," *Record of the 1973 IEEE Symposium on Computer Software Reliability.* New York: IEEE, 1973, pp. 78–81.

DEBUGGING EXPERIMENTS

One might also expect that a significant number of experiments have been performed in the area of program debugging, but again this is not the case. One of the few published debugging experiments [1, 2] involved programmers who were given Fortran subroutines, told that each contains a one-statement error, and asked to find the error. In some cases they were given additional aids, such as the expected versus actual output. None of the aids proved beneficial; the programmers who simply read through the program's logic fared as well as those who used aids. Another experiment [3] analyzed whether a programmer would be more or less effective in debugging a program than the program's original programmer—no difference was found.

REFERENCES

1. J. D. Gould and P. Drongowski, "An Exploratory Study of Computer Program Debugging," *Human Factors*, 16(3), 258–277 (1974).
2. J. D. Gould, "Some Psychological Evidence on how People Debug Computer Programs," *Int. J. Man-Machine Studies*, 7(2), 151–182 (1975).
3. J. D. Musa, "An Exploratory Experiment with 'Foreign' Debugging of Programs," *Proceedings of the Symposium on Computer Software Engineering.* New York: Polytechnic, 1976, pp. 499–511.

INTERACTIVE DEBUGGING TOOLS

Many timesharing systems provide a set of standard debugging facilities, for instance, allowing the programmer to display storage from a terminal and set breakpoints (points in the program at which execution will be suspended when executed). As illustrations of more advanced tools, the EXDAMS system [1] gives the user the illusion of interacting with his or her program while it is executing, but EXDAMS actually executes the program first and builds a history file of the program's state changes during execution. When the user debugs the program, the program is "executed" through a playback of the history file. Because of the existence of the history file, EXDAMS can support such debugging requests as "show me the statement that set variable I to 0.5," "execute the program in the reverse direction," and "display a map showing all alterations, as the program executes, to variable A."

ISMS [2] functions in a similar way. The user selects the events (e.g., subroutine calls, modifications to variables) to be monitored in his Algol program and the sections of the program to be monitored. ISMS then executes the program and builds a data base of its execution history. The user can then view the program as a motion picture, watching its data flow or control flow in a forward or backward direction.

The CAPS system [3] provides a run-time environment for PL/I, Fortran, and Cobol programs. CAPS obtains control when a system-detected error occurs (e.g., division by 0, out-of-bounds subscript). CAPS then "reverse executes" the program, looking for the troublesome assignment statement that may have resulted in the failure. Unlike most systems, where the user is the active element and the tool is passive, CAPS reverses it; it controls the debugging process, asking the user for guidance where necessary.

REFERENCES

1. R. M. Balzer, "EXDAMS—Extendable Debugging and Monitoring System," *Proceedings of the 1969 Spring Joint Computer Conference.* Montvale, N.J.: AFIPS Press, 1969, pp. 567–580.
2. R. E. Fairly, "An Experimental Program-Testing Facility," *IEEE Trans. Software Eng.,* SE-1(4), 350–357 (1975).
3. T. R. Wilcox, A. M. Davis, and M. H. Tindall, "The Design and Implementation of a Table Driven, Interactive Diagnostic Programming System," *Commun. ACM,* 19(11), 609–616 (1976).

4. P. T. Brady, "Writing an Online Debugging Program for the Experienced User," *Commun. ACM*, 11(6), 423–427 (1968).

5. B. L. Wolman, "Debugging PL/I Programs in the Multics Environment," *Proceedings of the 1972 Fall Joint Computer Conference*. Montvale, N.J.: AFIPS Press, 1972, pp. 507–514.

COMPILER DEBUGGING AIDS

Many implementations of compilers for such languages as Fortran, Cobol, and PL/I contain debugging features added to the language. For instance, two debugging features were added to Cobol when defining the 1974 standard [1]: (1) the ability to designate arbitrary statements as debugging statements and to activate or deactivate them at compilation or run time, and (2) traps to debugging sections when certain events occur (e.g., procedure invocations, data references, file references).

Proposals [2–4] have been made to add a debugging statement of the form

ASSERT <boolean expression> statement

to languages. If the Boolean expression is *false,* the associated statment executes and the program is terminated immediately. Also, although not normally considered a debugging aid, there have been proposals for compilers that perform many more runtime semantic-error checks than current compilers perform [5–7].

REFERENCES

1. G. N. Baird, "Program Debugging using Cobol '74," *Proceedings of the 1975 National Computer Conference*. Montvale, N.J.: AFIPS Press, 1975, pp. 313–318.

2. D. Matuszek, "The Case for the ASSERT Statement," *SIGPLAN Not.*, 11(8) 3€ –37 (1976).

3. A. Pyster, "Using Assertions to Improve Language Translators," *Proceedings of the 1977 National Computer Conference*. Montvale, N.J.: AFIPS Press, pp. 665–668.

4. E. Satterthwaite, "Debugging Tools for High Level Languages," *Software Prac. & Exper*, 2(3), 197–217 (1972).

5. C. M. Thomson, "Error Checking, Tracing, and Dumping in an Algol 68 Checkout Compiler," *SIGPLAN Not.*, 12(7), 106–111 (1977).

6. C. N. Fischer and R. J. LeBlanc, "Efficient Implementation and Optimization of Run-Time Checking in PASCAL," *Proceedings of an ACM Conference on Language Design for Reliable Software*. New York: ACM, 1977, pp. 19–24.

7. M. V. Zelkowitz, P. R. McMullin, K. R. Merkel, and H.. J. Larsen, "Error Checking with Pointer Variables," *Proceedings of the 1976 ACM Annual Conference.* New York: ACM, 1976, pp. 391–395.
8. R. W. Conway and T. R. Wilcox, "Design and Implementation of a Diagnostic Compiler for PL/I," *Commun. ACM,* 16(3), 169–179 (1973).

PROGRAM STATE MONITORS

Program state monitors are similar to test-coverage monitors (in fact, one often sees both functions in a single tool), but a program state monitor is primarily a debugging, rather than testing, aid. It monitors a program during execution, watching for the arrival of certain predefined conditions and/or collecting data that would be useful during debugging. The PET monitor [1] prints a report specifying, for each assignment statement, the first, last, minimum, and maximum values assigned during execution and, for each DO-loop control variable, its minimum and maximum values. It also has a powerful assertion-checking facility. For instance, if one places the statement

ASSERT A(I) $\neq$ A(J) FOR ALL (I, J) (1:8) WHERE (I$\neq$J) LIMIT 2 VIOLATIONS HALT

in a program, the program will terminate the second time that the first eight elements of array A are not all different when this statement is executed.

The ACES monitor [2] allows the user to specify valid ranges for designated variables. If one of these variables is assigned a value outside of the specified range, an error is reported to the user.

REFERENCES

1. L. G. Stucki, "New Directions in Automated Tools for Improving Software Quality," *in* R. T. Yeh, ed., *Current Trends in Programming Methodology, Volume II, Program Validation.* Englewood Cliffs, N.J.: Prentice-Hall, 1977, pp. 80–111.
2. C. V. Ramamoorthy, R. E. Meeker, and J. Turner, "Design and Construction of an Automated Software Evaluation System," *Record of the 1973 IEEE Symposium on Computer Software Reliability.* New York: IEEE, 1973, pp. 28–37.

COMPUTER ARCHITECTURE

A final interesting aid is the concept of designing the architecture of the underlying machine to assist the testing and debug-

ging processes. Ehrman [1] expresses the opinion that many programming and debugging difficulties are caused by poor
computer design, and that the costs of inadequate hardware design are passed on to the user in the form of higher debugging
costs of software. His recommendations include (1) a physical
identification of undefined (unset) storage words to allow the machine to detect references to uninitialized variables; (2) a set of
tag bits attached to each word, describing its content/attributes,
to allow the machine to detect meaningless operations; and (3) a
hardware mechanism to check argument/parameter consistency
during subroutine calls.

The SWARD (software-reliability-directed) machine architecture [2–4] employs these ideas and others. Its design objectives
were to detect many types of semantic errors whose detection by
compiler-generated code is too costly, to limit the consequences
of errors when they occur, and to facilitate the use of debugging
and testing tools. Other proposals have the machine detecting
invalid module-call sequences [5] and tracing the last n branch
instructions and state changes to assist the debugging process
[6].

REFERENCES

1. J. R. Ehrman, "System Design, Machine Architecture, and Debugging," *SIG-
   PLAN Not.,* 7(8), 8–23 (1972).

2. G. J. Myers, "The Design of Computer Architectures to Enhance Software
   Reliability," Ph.D. dissertation, Polytechnic Institute of New York, 1977.

3. G. J. Myers, *Advances in Computer Architecture.* New York: Wiley–Interscience, 1978, Chapters 13–15.

4. G. J. Myers, "Storage Concepts in a Software-Reliability-Directed Computer
   Architecture," *Proceedings of the Fifth Annual Symposium on Computer
   Architecture.* New York: ACM, 1978, pp. 107–113.

5. J. R. Kane and S. S. Yau, "Concurrent Software Fault Detection," *IEEE
   Trans. Software Eng.* SE-1(1), 87–99 (1975).

6. H. J. Saul and L. J. Shustek, "On Measuring Computer Systems by Microprogramming," *Microprogramming and Systems Architecture: Infotech State of
   the Art Report 23.* Berkshire, England: Infotech, 1975, pp. 473–489.

A NOTE ON THE REFERENCES

Most of the references in this chapter should be available in
any good technical library. A few of the conference proceedings
may not be widely available in libraries. Those published by the
ACM can be purchased from the Association for Computing

Machinery, 1133 Avenue of the Americas, New York, N.Y. 10036. The proceedings published by the IEEE can be ordered from the IEEE Service Center, 445 Hoes Lane, Piscataway, N.J. 08854. The periodicals *Data Base, SIGPLAN Notices,* and *Software Engineering Notes* are published by ACM special-interest groups.

The references from private organizations (companies and universities) can usually be obtained by writing to the organizations. Dissertations can be ordered from University Microfilms, 300 North Zeeb Road, Ann Arbor, Michgan 48106, Documents with NTIS numbers can be purchased from the National Technical Information Service, U.S. Department of Commerce, 5285 Port Royal Road, Springfield, Virginia 22161.

Index